SAVED BY GRACE

John Bunyan

Vintage Puritan Series
GLH Publishing
Louisville, KY

Originally Titled *Saved by Grace; or, A Discourse of the Grace of God*. Edited by George Offor. Blackie and Son: Glasgow, 1853.

GLH Publishing Reprint, 2020

ISBN:
  Paperback 978-1-948648-94-3
  Epub 978-1-948648-95-0

*Sign up for updates from GLH Publishing
using the link below and receive a free ebook.*
http://eepurl.com/gj9V19

Contents

Preface 1

Introduction 2

Question I. 5
                   What is it to be saved?

Question II. 22
                What is it to be saved by grace?

Question III. 36
           Who are they that are to be saved by grace?

Question IV. 41
     How it appears that they that are saved, are saved by grace?

Question V. 56
    What might be the reason moved God to ordain and choose to save those that he saveth by his grace, rather than by any other means?

Postscript 61

Preface

Courteous Reader,

In this little book thou art presented with a discourse of the GRACE of God, and of salvation by that grace. In which discourse, thou shalt find how each Person in the Godhead doth his part in the salvation of the sinner. I. The Father putteth forth his grace, thus. II. The Son putteth forth his grace, thus. III. And the Spirit putteth forth his grace, thus. Which things thou shalt find here particularly handled.

Thou shalt also find, in this small treatise, the way of God with the sinner, as to his CONVERSATION,[1] and the way of the sinner with God in the same; where[in] the grace of God, and the wickedness of the sinner, do greatly show themselves.

If thou findest me short in things, impute that [to] my love to brevity. If thou findest me besides the truth in aught, impute that to mine infirmity. But if thou findest anything here that serveth to thy furtherance and joy of faith, impute that to the mercy of God bestowed on thee and me.

Thine to serve thee with that little I have,
    John Bunyan.

---

1 General course of manners, behaviour, deportment, especially as it regards morals (see Phil. i. 27, 1 Peter i. 15).

Introduction

By grace ye are saved.
Ephesians ii. 5.

In the first chapter, from the fourth to the twelfth verse, the apostle is treating of the doctrine of election, both with respect to the act itself, the end, and means conducing thereto. The act, he tells us, was God's free choice of some (verse 4, 5, 11). The end was God's glory in their salvation (verse 6, 14). The means conducing to that end was Jesus Christ himself—'In whom we have redemption through his blood, the forgiveness of sins, according to the riches of his grace' (verse 7). This done, he treateth of the subjection of the Ephesians to the faith, as it was held forth to them in the Word of the truth of the gospel, as also of their being sealed by the Holy Spirit of God unto the day of redemption (verse 12-14). Moreover, he telleth them how he gave thanks to God for them, making mention of them in his prayers, even that he would make them see 'what is the hope of his calling, and what the riches of the glory of his inheritance in the saints, and what is the exceeding greatness of his power to usward who believe, according to the working of his mighty power, which he wrought in Christ, when he raised him from the dead,' &c. (verse 15-20).

And lest the Ephesians, at the hearing of these their so many privileges, should forget how little they deserved them, he tells them that in time past they were dead in trespasses and sins, and that then they walked in them 'according to the course of this world, according to the prince of the power of the air, the spirit that now worketh in the children of disobedience' (Eph. ii. 2, 3).

Having thus called them back to the remembrance of themselves—to wit, what they were in their state of unregeneracy, he proceedeth to show them that their first quickening was by the resurrection of Christ their Head, in whom they before were chosen, and that by him they were already set down in heavenly places, (verse 5, 6); inserting, by the way, the true cause of all this blessedness, with what else should be by us enjoyed in another world; and that is, the love and grace of God: 'But God, who is rich in mercy, for his great love wherewith he loved us, even when we were dead in sins, hath quickened us together with Christ [by grace ye are saved].' These last words seen to be the apostle's conclusion rightly drawn from the premises; as who should say, If you Ephesians were indeed dead in trespasses and sins; if indeed you were by nature the children of wrath, even as others, then you deserve no more than others.[2]

Again, if God hath chosen you, if God hath justified and saved you by his Christ, and left others as good as you by nature to perish in their sins, then the true cause of this your blessed condition is, the free grace of God. But just thus it is, therefore by grace ye are saved; therefore all the good which you enjoy more than others, it is of mere goodwill.

'BY GRACE YE ARE SAVED.'

The method that I shall choose to discourse upon these words shall be this—I will propound certain questions

---

[2] Their conduct proved to the living that they were dead, they themselves having no feeling or sense of spiritual life; but, when quickened, their penitence and good works were brought into existence by Divine power; they feel the joys of salvation, but feel also their total unworthiness of this new creating power, and sing, 'O to grace how great a debtor!'—ED.

upon the words, and direct particular answers to them; in which answers I hope I shall answer also, somewhat at least, the expectation of the godly and conscientious reader, and so shall draw towards a conclusion.

THE QUESTIONS ARE—

I. What is it to be saved?

II. What is it to be saved by grace?

III. Who are they that are saved by grace?

IV. How it appears that they that are saved, are saved by grace?

V. What might be the reasons which prevailed with God to save us by grace, rather than by any other means?

Now the reason why I propound these five questions upon the words, it is, because the words themselves admit them; the first three are grounded upon the several phrases in the text, and the two last are to make way for demonstration of the whole.

QUESTION I.

WHAT IS IT TO BE SAVED?

This question supposeth that there is such a thing as damnation due to man for sin; for to save supposeth the person to be saved to be at present in a sad condition; saving, to him that is not lost, signifies nothing, neither is it anything in itself. 'To save, to redeem, to deliver,' are in the general terms equivalent, and they do all of them suppose us to be in a state of thraldom and misery; therefore this word 'saved,' in the sense that the apostle here doth use it, is a word of great worth, forasmuch as the miseries from which we are saved is the misery of all most dreadful.

The miseries from which they that shall be saved shall by their salvation be delivered, are dreadful; they are no less than sin, the curse of God, and flames of hell for ever. What more abominable than sin? What more insupportable than the dreadful wrath of an angry God? And what more fearful than the bottomless pit of hell? I say, what more fearful than to be tormented there for ever with the devil and his angels? Now, to 'save,' according to my text, is to deliver the sinner from these, with all things else that attend them. And although sinners may think that it is no hard matter to answer this question, yet I must tell you there is no man, that can feelingly know what it is to be saved, that knoweth not experimentally something of the dread of these three things, as is evident, because all others do even by their practice count it a thing of no great concern, when yet it is of all other of the highest concern among men; 'For what is a man profited if he shall gain the whole world, and lose his own soul?' (Matt. xvi. 26).

But, I say, if this word 'saved' concludeth our deliverance from sin, how can he tell what it is to be saved that hath not in his conscience groaned under the burden of sin? yea, it is impossible else that he should ever cry out with all his heart, 'Men and brethren, what shall we do?'—that is, do to be saved (Acts ii. 37). The man that hath no sores or aches cannot know the virtue of the salve; I mean, not know it from his own experience, and therefore cannot prize, nor have that esteem of it, as he that hath received cure thereby. Clap a plaster to a well place, and that maketh not its virtue to appear; neither can he to whose flesh it is so applied, by that application understand its worth. Sinners, you, I mean, that are not wounded with guilt, and oppressed with the burden of sin, you cannot—I will say it again—you cannot know, in this senseless condition of yours, what it is to be saved.

Again; this word 'saved,' as I said, concludeth deliverance from the wrath of God. How, then, can he tell what it is to be saved that hath not felt the burden of the wrath of God? He—he that is astonished with, and that trembleth at, the wrath of God—he knows best what it is to be saved (Acts xvi. 29).

Further, this word 'saved,' it concludeth deliverance from death and hell. How, then, can he tell what it is to be saved that never was sensible of the sorrows of the one, nor distressed with the pains of the other? The Psalmist says, 'The sorrows of death compassed me, and the pains of hell gat hold upon me: I found trouble and sorrow. Then called I upon the name of the Lord'— (mark, then), 'then called I upon the name of the Lord; O Lord, I beseech thee, deliver my soul,'—then, in my distress. When he knew what it was to be saved, then he called, because, I say, then he knew what it was to be saved (Psa. xviii. 4, 5; cxvi. 3, 4). I say, this is the man, and this only, that knows what it is to be saved. And this is evident, as is manifest by the little regard that the rest have to saving, or the little dread they have of damnation. Where is he that seeks and groans for salvation? I say, where is he that hath taken his flight for salvation, because of the dread of the wrath to come? 'O generation of vipers, who hath warned you to flee from the wrath to come?' (Matt. iii. 7). Alas! do not the most set light by salvation?—as for sin, how do they love it, embrace it, please themselves with it, hide it still within their mouth, and keep it close under their tongue. Besides, for the wrath of God, they feel it not, they fly not from it; and for hell, it is become a doubt to many if there be any, and a mock to those whose doubt is resolved by atheism.

But to come to the question—What is it to be saved? To be saved may either respect salvation in the whole of it, or salvation in the parts of it, or both. I think this text respecteth both—to wit, salvation completing, and salvation completed; for 'to save' is a work of many steps; or, to be as plain as possible, 'to save' is a work that hath its beginning before the world began, and shall not be completed before it is ended.

First, then, we may be said to be saved in the purpose of God before the world began. The apostle saith that 'he saved us, and called us with an holy calling, not according to our works, but according to his own purpose and grace, which was given us in Christ Jesus before the world began' (2 Tim. i. 9). This is the beginning of salvation, and according to this beginning all things concur and fall out in conclusion—'He hath saved us according to his eternal purpose, which he purposed in Christ Jesus.' God in thus saving may be said to save us by determining to make those means effectual for the blessed completing of our salvation; and hence we are said 'to be chosen in Christ to salvation.' And again, that he hath in that choice given us that grace that shall complete our salvation. Yea, the text is very full, 'He hath blessed us with all spiritual blessings in heavenly places in Christ, according as he hath chosen us in him before the foundation of the world' (Eph. i. 3, 4).

Second. As we may be said to be saved in the purpose of God before the foundation of the world, so we may be said to be saved before we are converted, or called to Christ. And hence 'saved' is put before 'called'; 'he hath saved us, and called us'; he saith not, he hath called us, and saved us; but he puts saving before calling (2 Tim. i. 9). So again, we are said to be 'preserved in Christ and called'; he saith not, called and preserved (Jude 1). And therefore God saith again, 'I will pardon them whom I reserve' — that is, as Paul expounds it, those whom I have 'elected and kept,' and this part of salvation is accomplished through the forbearance of God (Jer. l. 20; Rom. xi. 4, 5). God beareth with is own elect, for Christ's sake, all the time of their unregeneracy, until the time comes which he hath appointed for their conversion. The sins that we stood guilty of before conversion, had the judgment due to them been executed upon us, we had not now been in the world to partake of a heavenly calling. But the judgment due to them hath been by the patience of God prevented, and we saved all the time of our ungodly and unconverted state, from that death, and those many hells, that for our sins we deserved at the hands of God.

And here lies the reason that long life is granted to the elect before conversion, and that all the sins they commit and all the judgments they deserve, cannot drive them out of the world before conversion. Manasseh, you know, was a great sinner, and for the trespass which he committed he was driven from his own land, and carried to Babylon; but kill him they could not, though his sins had deserved death ten thousand times. But what was the reason? Why, he was not yet called; God had chosen him in Christ, and laid up in him a stock of grace, which must be given to Manasseh before he dies; therefore Manasseh must be convinced, converted, and saved. That legion of devils that was in the possessed, with all the sins which he had committed in the time of his unregeneracy, could not take away his life before his conversion (Mark v.). How many times was that poor creature, as we may easily conjecture, assaulted for his life by the devils that were in him, yet could they not kill him, yea, though his dwelling was near the sea-side, and the devils had power to drive him too, yet could they not drive him further than the mountains that were by the sea- side; yea, they could help him often to break his chains and fetters, and could also make him as mad as a bedlam,[3] they could also prevail with him to separate from men, and cut himself with stones, but kill him they could not, drown him they could not; he was saved to be called; he was, notwithstanding all this, preserved in Christ, and called. As it is said of the young lad in the gospel, he was by the devil cast oft into the fire, and oft into the water, to destroy him, but it could not be; even so hath he served others, but they must be 'saved to be called' (Mark ix. 22). How many deaths have some been delivered from and saved out of before conversion! Some have fallen into rivers, some into wells, some into the sea, some into the hands of men; yea, they have been justly arraigned and condemned, as the thief upon the cross, but must not die before they have been converted. They were preserved in Christ, and called.

Called Christian, how many times have thy sins laid thee upon a sick- bed, and, to thine and others' thinking, at the very mouth of the grave? yet God said concerning thee, Let him live, for he is not yet converted. Behold, therefore, that the elect are saved before they are called.[4] 'God, who is rich in mercy, for his great

---

3 The hospital of St. Mary Bethlem, vulgarly called 'Bedlam,' bestowed, in 1545, upon the citizens of London, who appropriated it to the reception of lunatics. It being the only public hospital for that class of the afflicted in England, it gave the name of 'bedlam' to all whose conduct could only be accounted for on the score of madness.—ED.

4 The person who writes this, was a singular instance of the truth of our author's remark; having been twice providentially pre-

love wherewith he loved us, even when we were dead in sins,' hath preserved us in Christ, and called us (Eph. ii. 4, 5).

Now this 'saving' of us arises from six causes. 1. God hath chosen us unto salvation, and therefore will not frustrate his own purposes (1 Thess. v. 9). 2. God hath given us to Christ; and his gift, as well as his calling, is without repentance (Rom. xi. 29; John vi. 37). 3. Christ hath purchased us with his blood (Rom. v. 8, 9). 4. They are, by God, counted in Christ before they are converted (Eph. i. 3, 4). 5. They are ordained before conversion to eternal life; yea, to be called, to be justified, to be glorified, and therefore all this must come upon them (Rom. viii. 29, 30). 6. For all this, he hath also appointed them their portion and measure of grace, and that before the world began; therefore, that they may partake of all these privileges, they are saved and called, preserved in Christ, and called.

Third. To be saved is to be brought to, and helped to lay hold on, Jesus Christ by faith. And this is called saving by grace through faith. 'For by grace are ye saved through faith; and that not of yourselves, it is the gift of God' (Eph. ii. 8).

1. They must be brought unto Christ, yea, drawn unto him; for 'no man,' saith Christ, 'can come to me, except the Father which hath sent me draw him' (John

---

served from drowning, and once from the fatal effects of a violent fever, before effectual saving grace had reached his soul. The same rich and abundant mercy follows all the elect, quickens them when dead, saves them when lost, and restores them when ruined. God hath chosen us unto salvation, and enables us to live holily on earth, in order to a life of happiness in heaven. The Father's good will and pleasure is the only fountain from whence the salvation of believers flows; and such as are given to Christ by the Father he considers as his charge, and stands engaged for their preservation; and the death of Christ for sinners, is an evident demonstration of the love of God the Father, and the Lord Jesus Christ, towards them; this love manifested in time was in and upon the heart of God before the world began. — Mason. What a multitude of unseen dangers, both spiritual and temporal, the Christian escapes before he is called! — ED.

vi. 44). Men, even the elect, have too many infirmities to come to Christ without help from heaven; inviting will not do. 'As they called them, so they went from them,' therefore he 'drew them with cords' (Hosea xi. 2, 4).

2. As they must be brought to, so they must be helped to lay hold on Christ by faith; for as coming to Christ, so faith, is not in our own power; therefore we are said to be raised up with him 'through the faith of the operation of God.' And again, we are said to believe, 'according to the working of his mighty power, which he wrought in Christ, when he raised him from the dead' (Col. ii. 12; Eph. i. 19, 20). Now we are said to be saved by faith, because by faith we lay hold of, venture upon, and put on Jesus Christ for life. For life, I say, because God having made him the Saviour, hath given him life to communicate to sinners, and the life that he communicates to them is the merit of his flesh and blood, which whoso eateth and drinketh by faith, hath eternal life, because that flesh and blood hath merit in it sufficient to obtain the favour of God. Yea, it hath done so [since] that day it was offered through the eternal Spirit a sacrifice of a sweet-smelling savour to him; wherefore God imputeth the righteousness of Christ to him that believeth in him, by which righteousness he is personally justified, and saved from that just judgment of the law that was due unto him (John v. 26, vi. 53-58; Eph. iv. 32; v. 2; Rom. iv. 23-25).

'Saved by faith.' For although salvation beginneth in God's purpose, and comes to us through Christ's righteousness, yet is not faith exempted from having a hand in saving of us. Not that it meriteth aught, but is given by God to those which he saveth, that thereby they may embrace and put on that Christ by whose righteousness they must be saved. Wherefore this faith is that which here distinguisheth them that shall be saved from them that shall be damned. Hence it is said, 'He that believeth not, shall be damned'; and hence again it is that the believers are called 'the children, the heirs, and the blessed with faithful Abraham;' that the promise by faith in Jesus Christ might be given to them that believe (Gal. iii. 6-9, 26; Rom. iv. 13, 14).

And here let Christians warily distinguish betwixt the meritorious and the instrumental cause of their justification. Christ, with what he hath done and suffered, is the meritorious cause of our justification; therefore he is said to be made to us of God, 'wisdom and righteousness;' and we are said to be 'justified by his blood, and saved from wrath through him,' for it was his life and blood that were the price of our redemption (1 Cor. i. 30; Rom. v. 9, 10). 'Redeemed,' says Peter, 'not with corruptible things, as silver and gold,' alluding to the redemption of money under the law, 'but with the precious blood of Christ.' Thou art, therefore, as I have said, to make Christ Jesus the object of thy faith for justification; for by his righteousness thy sins must be covered from the sight of the justice of the law. 'Believe on the Lord Jesus Christ, and thou shalt be saved.' 'For he shall save his people from their sins' (Acts xvi. 31; Matt. i. 21).

Fourth. To be saved is to be preserved in the faith to the end. 'He that shall endure unto the end, the same shall be saved' (Matt. xxiv. 13). Not that perseverance is an accident in Christianity, or a thing performed by human industry; they that are saved 'are kept by the power of God, through faith unto salvation' (1 Peter i. 3-6).

But perseverance is absolutely necessary to the complete saving of the soul, because he that falleth short of the state that they that are saved are possessed of, as saved, cannot arrive to that saved state. He that goeth to sea with a purpose to arrive at Spain, cannot arrive there if he be drowned by the way; wherefore perseverance is absolutely necessary to the saving of the soul, and therefore it is included in the complete saving of us—'Israel shall be saved in the Lord with an everlasting salvation: ye shall not be ashamed nor confounded world without end' (Isa. xlv. 17). Perseverance is here made absolutely necessary to the complete saving of the soul.

But, as I said, this part of salvation dependeth not upon human power, but upon him that hath begun a good work in us (Phil. i. 6). This part, therefore, of our salvation is great, and calleth for no less than the power of God for our help to perform it, as will be easily granted by all those that consider—

1. That all the power and policy, malice and rage, of the devils and hell itself are against us. Any man that understandeth this will conclude that to be saved is no small thing. The devil is called a god, a prince, a lion, a roaring lion; it is said that he hath death and the power of it, &c. But what can a poor creature, whose habitation is in flesh, do against a god, a prince, a roaring lion, and the power of death itself? Our perseverance, therefore, lieth in the power of God; 'the gates of hell shall not prevail against it.'

2. All the world is against him that shall be saved. But what is one poor creature to all the world, especially if you consider that with the world is terror, fear, power, majesty, laws, jails, gibbets, hangings, burnings, drownings, starvings, banishments, and a thousand kinds of deaths? (1 John v. 4, 5; John xvi. 33).

3. Add to this, that all the corruptions that dwell in our flesh are against us, and that not only in their nature and being, but they lust against us, and war against us, to 'bring us into captivity to the law of sin and death' (Gal. v. 17; 1 Peter ii. 11; Rom. vii. 23).

4. All the delusions in the world are against them that shall be saved, many of which are so cunningly woven, so plausibly handled, so rarely[5] polished with Scripture and reason, that it is ten thousand wonders that the elect are not swallowed up with them; and swallowed up they would be, were they not elect, and was not God himself engaged, either by power to keep them from falling, or by grace to pardon if they fall, and to lift them up again (Matt. xxiv. 24; Eph. iv. 14; Rom. iii. 12).

5. Every fall of the saved is against the salvation

---

5 'Rarely,' finely, nicely.

of his soul; but a Christian once fallen riseth not but as helped by Omnipotent power— 'O Israel, thou hast fallen by thine iniquity,' 'but in me is thy help,' says God (Hosea xiii. 9; xiv. 1; Psa. xxxvii. 23).

Christians, were you awake, here would be matter of wonder to you, to see a man assaulted with all the power of hell, and yet to come off a conqueror! Is it not a wonder to see a poor creature, who in himself is weaker than the moth, to stand against and overcome all devils, all the world, all his lusts and corruptions? (Job iv. 19). Or if he fall, is it not a wonder to see him, when devils and guilt are upon him, to rise again, stand upon his feet again, walk with God again, and persevere after all this in the faith and holiness of the gospel? He that knows himself, wonders; he that knows temptation, wonders; he that knows what falls and guilt mean, wonders; indeed, perseverance is a wonderful thing, and is managed by the power of God; for he only 'is able to keep you from falling, and to present you faultless before the presence of his glory with exceeding joy' (Jude 24). Those of the children of Israel that went from Egypt, and entered the land of Canaan, how came they thither? Why, the text says, that 'as an eagle spreadeth abroad her wings, so the Lord alone did lead them.' And again, 'he bore them, and carried them all the days of old' (Deut. xxxii. 11, 12; Isa. lxiii. 9). David also tells us that mercy and goodness should follow him all the days of his life, and so he should dwell in the house of the Lord for ever (Psa. xxiii. 6).

Fifth. To be saved calls for more than all this; he that is saved, must, when this world can hold him no longer, have a safe-conduct to heaven, for that is the place where they that are saved must to the full enjoy their salvation. This heaven is called 'the end of our faith,' because it is that which faith looks at; as Peter says, 'Receiving the end of your faith, even the salvation of your souls.' And again, 'But we are not of them who draw back unto perdition; but of them that believe to the saving of the soul' (1 Peter i. 9; Heb. x. 39). For, as I said, heaven is the place for the saved to enjoy their salvation in, with that perfect gladness that is not attainable here. Here we are saved by faith and hope of glory; but there, we that are saved shall enjoy the end of our faith and hope, even the salvation of our souls. There is 'Mount Zion, the heavenly Jerusalem, the general assembly and church of the firstborn;' there is the 'innumerable company of angels, and the spirits of just men made perfect;' there is 'God the judge of all, and Jesus the Mediator of the new covenant;' there shall our soul have as much of heaven as it is capable of enjoying, and that without intermission; wherefore, when we come there we shall be saved indeed! But now for a poor creature to be brought hither, this is the life of the point. But how shall I come hither? there are heights and depths to hinder (Rom. viii. 38, 39).

Suppose the poor Christian is now upon a sick-bed, beset with a thousand fears, and ten thousand at the end of that; sick-bed fears! and they are sometimes dreadful ones; fears that are begotten by the review of the sin, perhaps, of forty years' profession; fears that are begotten by dreadful and fearful suggestions of the devil, the sight of death, and the grave, and it may be of hell itself; fears that are begotten by the withdrawing and silence of God and Christ, and by, it may be, the appearance of the devil himself; some of these made David cry, 'O spare me' a little, 'that I may recover strength before I go hence, and be no more' (Psa. xxxix. 13). 'The sorrows of death,' said he, 'compassed me, and the pains of hell gat hold upon me; I found trouble and sorrow' (Psa. cxvi. 3). These things, in another place, he calls the bands that the godly have in their death, and the plagues that others are not aware of. 'They are not in trouble as other men; neither are they plagued like other men' (Psa. lxxiii. 9). But now, out of all these, the Lord will save his people; not one sin, nor fear, nor devil shall hinder; nor the grave nor hell disappoint thee. But how must this be? Why, thou must have a safe-conduct to heaven?[6] What conduct? A conduct of angels: 'Are they not all ministering spirits, sent forth to minister for them who shall be heirs of salvation?' (Heb. i. 14).

These angels, therefore, are not to fail them that are the saved; but must, as commissioned of God, come down from heaven to do this office for them; they must come, I say, and take the care and charge of our soul, to conduct it safely into Abraham's bosom. It is not our meanness in the world, nor our weakness of faith, that shall hinder this; nor shall the loathsomeness of our diseases make these delicate spirits shy of taking this charge upon them. Lazarus the beggar found this a truth; a beggar so despised of the rich glutton that he was not suffered to come within his gate; a beggar full of sores and noisome putrefaction; yet, behold, when he dies, the angels come from heaven to fetch him thither: 'And it came to pass that the beggar died, and was carried by the angels into Abraham's bosom'[7] (Luke xvi. 22). True, sick-bed temptations are ofttimes the most violent, because then the devil plays his last game with us, he is never to assault us more; besides, perhaps God suffereth it thus to be, that the entering into heaven may be the sweeter, and ring of this salvation the louder! O it is a blessed thing for God to be our God and our guide even unto death, and then for his angels to conduct us safely to glory; this is saving indeed. And he shall save Israel 'out of all his troubles;' out of sick-bed troubles as well as others (Psa. xxv. 22; xxxiv. 6; xlviii. 14).

Sixth. To be saved, to be perfectly saved, calls for more than all this; the godly are not perfectly saved

---

6 A safe-conduct is a military term, either a convoy or guard for protection in an enemy's land, or a passport, by the sovereign of a country, to enable a subject to travel with safety.—Imperial Dict.— Ed.

7 What amazing love! Christ visited this poor beggar, yea, was formed in him the hope off glory; his body, so miserable in the sight of man, was a temple of the Holy Ghost, and the angels carry his soul to heaven. O the riches of grace!—Ed

when their soul is possessed of heaven. True, their spirit is made perfect, and hath as much of heaven as at present it can hold, but man, consisting of body and soul, cannot be said to be perfectly saved so long as but part of him is in the heavens; his body is the price of the blood of Christ as well as his spirit; his body is the temple of God, and a member of the body, and of the flesh, and of the bones of Christ; he cannot, then, be completely saved until the time of the resurrection of the dead (1 Cor. vi. 13-19; Eph. v. 30). Wherefore, when Christ shall come the second time, then will he save the body from all those things that at present make it incapable of the heavens. 'For our conversation is in heaven; from whence also we look for the Saviour, the Lord Jesus Christ; who shall change' this 'our vile body, that it may be fashioned like unto his glorious body' (Phil. iii. 20, 21). O what a great deal of good God hath put into this little word 'saved'! We shall not see all the good that God hath put into this word 'saved' until the Lord Jesus comes to raise the dead. 'It doth not yet appear what we shall be' (1 John iii. 2). But till it appears what we shall be, we cannot see the bottom of this word 'saved.' True, we have the earnest of what we shall be, we have the Spirit of God, 'which is the earnest of our inheritance until the redemption of the purchased possession' (Eph. i. 14). The possession is our body—it is called 'a purchased possession,' because it is the price of blood; now the redemption of this purchased possession is the raising of it out of the grave, which raising is called the redemption of our body (Rom. viii. 23). And when this vile body is made like unto his glorious body, and this body and soul together possessed of the heavens, then shall we be every way saved.

There are three things from which this body must be saved—1. There is that sinful filth and vileness that yet dwells in it, under which we groan earnestly all our days (2 Cor. v. 1-3). 2. There is mortality, that subjecteth us to age, sickness, aches, pains, diseases, and death. 3. And there is the grave and death itself, for death is the last enemy that is to be destroyed. 'So when this corruptible shall have put on incorruption, and this mortal shall have put on immortality, then shall be brought to pass the saying that is written, Death is swallowed up in victory' (1 Cor. xv. 54). So then, when this comes to pass, then we shall be saved; then will salvation, in all the parts of it, meet together in our glory; then we shall be every way saved—saved in God's decree, saved in Christ's undertakings, saved by faith, saved in perseverance, saved in soul, and in body and soul together in the heavens, saved perfectly, everlastingly, gloriously.

Of the state of our body and soul in heaven.

Before I conclude my answer to the first question, I would discourse a little of the state of our body and soul in heaven, when we shall enjoy this blessed state of salvation.

First. Of the soul; it will then be filled in all the faculties of it with as much bliss and glory as ever it can hold.

1. The understanding shall then be perfect in knowledge—'Now we know but in part;' we know God, Christ, heaven, and glory, but in part; 'but when that which is perfect is come, then that which is in part shall be done away' (1 Cor. xiii. 10). Then shall we have perfect and everlasting visions of God, and that blessed one his Son Jesus Christ, a good thought of whom doth sometimes so fill us while in this world, that it causeth 'joy unspeakable and full of glory.' 2. Then shall our will and affections be ever in a burning flame of love to God and his Son Jesus Christ; our love here hath ups and downs, but there it shall be always perfect with that perfection which is not possible in this world to be enjoyed. 3. Then will our conscience have that peace and joy that neither tongue nor pen of men or angels can express. 4. Then will our memory be so enlarged to retain all things that happened to us in this world, so that with unspeakable aptness we shall call to mind

all God's providences, all Satan's malice, all our own weaknesses, all the rage of men, and how God made all work together for his glory and our good, to the everlasting ravishing of our hearts.

Second. For our body; it shall be raised in power, in incorruption, a spiritual body and glorious (1 Cor. xv. 44). The glory of which is set forth by several things—1. It is compared to 'the brightness of the firmament,' and to the shining of the stars 'for ever and ever' (Dan. xii. 3; 1 Cor. xv. 41, 42). 2. It is compared to the shining of the sun— 'Then shall the righteous shine forth as the sun in the kingdom of their Father. Who hath ears to hear, let him hear' (Matt. xiii. 43). 3. Their state is then to be equally glorious with angels; 'But they which shall be counted worthy to obtain that world, and the resurrection from the dead, neither marry, nor are given in marriage; neither can they die any more, for they are equal unto the angels' (Luke xx. 35, 36). 4. It is said that then this our vile body shall be like the glorious body of Jesus Christ (Phil. iii. 20, 21; 1 John iii. 2, 3). 5. And now, when body and soul are thus united, who can imagine what glory they both possess? They will now be both in capacity, without jarring, to serve the Lord with shouting thanksgivings, and with a crown of everlasting joy upon their head.[8]

In this world there cannot be that harmony and oneness of body and soul as there will be in heaven. Here the body sometimes sins against the soul, and the soul again vexes and perplexes the body with dreadful apprehensions of the wrath and judgment of God. While we be in this world, the body oft hangs this way, and the soul the quite contrary; but there, in heaven, they shall have that perfect union as never to jar more;

---

8 What heart can conceive the glorious worship of heaven? The new song shall be as the voice of many waters, and a great thunder, when the 'ten thousand times ten thousand and thousand of thousands' shall sing, 'Worthy is the Lamb that was slain, to receive power, and riches, and wisdom, and strength, and honour, and blessing.' O that my poor voice may join that celestial choir!—ED.

but now the glory of the body shall so suit with the glory of the soul, and both so perfectly suit with the heavenly state, that it passeth words and thoughts.

Third. Shall I now speak of the place that this saved body and soul shall dwell in?

Why, 1. It is a city (Heb. xi. 16; Eph. ii. 19, 22). 2. It is called heaven (Heb. x. 34). 3. It is called God's house (John xiv. 1-3). 4. It is called a kingdom (Luke xii. 32). 5. It is called glory (Col. iii. 4; Heb. ii. 10). 6. It is called paradise (Rev. ii. 7). 7. It is called everlasting habitations (Luke xvi. 9).

Fourth. Shall I speak of their company?

Why, 1. They shall stand and live in the presence of the glorious God, the Judge of all (Heb. xii. 23). 2. They shall be with the Lamb, the Lord Jesus. 3. They shall be with an innumerable company of holy angels (Heb. xii. 22). 4. They shall be with Abraham, Isaac, and Jacob, and all the prophets, in the kingdom of heaven (Luke xiii. 28).

Fifth. Shall I speak of their heavenly raiment?

1. It is salvation; they shall be clothed with the garment of salvation (Psa. cxxxii. 16; cxlix. 4; Isa. lxi. 10). 2. This raiment is called white raiment, signifying their clean and innocent state in heaven. 'And they,' says Christ, 'shall walk with me in white, for they are worthy' (Rev. iii. 4; xix. 8; Isa. lvii. 2). 3. It is called glory—'When he shall appear, we shall appear with him in glory' (Col. iii. 4). 4. They shall also have crowns of righteousness, everlasting joy and glory (Isa. xxxv. 10; 2 Tim. iv. 8; 1 Peter v. 4).

Sixth. Shall I speak of their continuance in this condition?

1. It is for ever and ever. 'And they shall see his face, and his name shall be in their foreheads; and they shall reign for ever and ever' (Rev. xxii. 4, 5). 2. It is everlasting. 'And this is the will of him that sent me, that every one which seeth the Son, and believeth on him, may have everlasting life' (John vi. 40, 47). 3. It is life eternal. 'My sheep hear my voice, and I know them, and they

follow me; and I give unto them eternal life' (John x. 27, 28). 4. It is world without end. 'But Israel shall be saved in the Lord with an everlasting salvation; ye shall not be ashamed nor confounded world without end' (Isa. xlv. 17; Eph. iii. 20, 21).

O sinner! what sayest thou? How dost thou like being saved? Doth not thy mouth water? Doth not thy heart twitter at being saved? Why, come then: 'The Spirit and the bride say, Come. And let him that heareth say, Come. And let him that is athirst come. And whosoever will, let him take the water of life freely' (Rev. xxii. 17).

Question II.

What is it to be saved by grace?

Now I come to the second question—to wit, What is it to be saved by grace? For so are the words of the text, 'By grace ye are saved.' But,

First. I must touch a little upon the word GRACE, and show you how diversely it is taken. Sometimes it is taken for the goodwill and favour of men (Esth. ii. 17: Ruth ii. 2: 1 Sam. i. 18: 2 Sam. xvi. 4). Sometimes it is taken for those sweet ornaments that a life according to the Word of God putteth about the neck[9] (Prov. i. 9; iii. 22). Sometimes it is taken for the charity of the saints, as 2 Corinthians ix. 6-8.

But 'grace' in the text is taken for God's goodwill, 'the goodwill of him that dwelt in the bush;' and is expressed variously. Sometimes it is called 'his good pleasure.' Sometimes, 'the good pleasure of his will,' which is all one with 'the riches of his grace' (Eph. i. 7). Sometimes it is expressed by goodness, pity, love, mercy, kindness, and the like (Rom. ii. 4; Isa. lxiii. 9; Titus iii. 4, 5). Yea, he styles himself, 'The Lord, the Lord God, merciful and gracious, long-suffering, and abundant in goodness and truth, keeping mercy for thousands, forgiving iniquity and transgression and sin, and that will

---

9   The fear of the Lord—an ornament of grace unto thy head, and chains about thy neck, and life unto thy soul.—Solomon.

QUESTION II.

by no means clear the guilty' (Exod. xxxiv. 6, 7).

Second. As the word 'grace' signifieth all these, so it intimates to us that all these are free acts of God, free love, free mercy, free kindness; hence we have other hints in the Word about the nature of grace, as, 1. It is an act of God's will, which must needs be free; an act of his own will, of the good pleasure of his will; by each of these expressions is intimated that grace is a free act of God's goodness towards the sons of men. 2. Therefore it is expressly said — 'Being justified freely by his grace' (Rom. iii. 24). 3. 'And when they had nothing to pay, he frankly forgave them both' (Luke vii. 42). 4. And again, 'Not for your sakes do I this, saith the Lord God, be it known unto you' (Ezek. xxxvi. 32; Deut. ix. 5). 5. And therefore 'grace,' and the deservings of the creature, are set in flat opposition one to another — 'And if by grace, then is it no more of works; otherwise grace is no more grace. But if it be of works, then is it no more grace; otherwise work is no more work' (Rom. xi. 6).

The word 'grace,' therefore, being understood, doth most properly set forth the true cause of man's happiness with God, not but that those expressions, love, mercy, goodness, pity, kindness, &c., and the like, have their proper place in our happiness also. Had not God loved us, grace had not acted freely in our salvation; had not God been merciful, good, pitiful, kind, he would have turned away from us when he saw us in our blood (Ezek. xvi.).

So then, when he saith, 'By grace ye are saved,' it is all one as if he had said, By the goodwill, free mercy, and loving-kindness of God ye are saved; as the words conjoined with the text do also further manifest: 'But God,' saith Paul, 'who is rich in mercy, for his great love wherewith he loved us, even when we were dead in sins, hath quickened us together with Christ [by grace ye are saved].'

[Third.] The words thus understood admit us these few conclusions — 1. That God, in saving of the sinner, hath no respect to the sinner's goodness; hence it is said he is frankly forgiven, and freely justified (Luke vii. 42; Rom. iii. 24). 2. That God doth this to whom and when he pleases, because it is an act of his own good pleasure (Gal. i. 15, 16). 3. This is the cause why great sinners are saved, for God pardoneth 'according to the riches of his grace' (Eph. i. 7). 4. This is the true cause that some sinners are so amazed and confounded at the apprehension of their own salvation; his grace is unsearchable; and by unsearchable grace God oft puzzles and confounds our reason (Ezek. xvi. 62, 63; Acts ix. 6). 5. This is the cause that sinners are so often recovered from their backslidings, healed of their wounds that they get by their falls, and helped again to rejoice in God's mercy. Why, he will be gracious to whom he will be gracious, and he will have compassion on whom he will have compassion (Rom. ix. 15).

[Fourth.] But I must not here conclude this point. We are here discoursing of the grace of God, and that by it we are saved; saved, I say, by the grace of God.

Now, God is set forth in the Word unto us under a double consideration—1. He is set forth in his own eternal power and Godhead; and as thus set forth, we are to conceive of him by his attributes of power, justice, goodness, holiness, everlastingness, &c. 2. But then, we have him set forth in the Word of truth as consisting of Father, Son, and Spirit; and although this second consideration containeth in it the nature of the Godhead, yet the first doth not demonstrate the persons in the Godhead. We are saved by the grace of God—that is, by the grace of the Father, who is God; by the grace of the Son, who is God; and by the grace of the Spirit, who is God.

Now, since we are said to be 'saved by grace,' and that the grace of God; and since also we find in the Word that in the Godhead there are Father, Son, and Holy Ghost, we must conclude that it is by the grace of the Father, Son, and Spirit that we are saved; wherefore grace is attributed to the Father, Son, and Holy Ghost distinctly. 1. Grace is attributed to the Father, as these scriptures testify; Romans vii. 25, 1 Corinthians i. 3, 2 Corinthians i. 2, Galatians i. 3, Ephesians i. 2, Philippians i. 2, Colossians i. 2, 1 Thessalonians i. 1, 2 Thessalonians i. 2, 1 Timothy i. 2, 2 Timothy i. 2, Titus i. 4, Philemon 3. 2. Grace is also attributed to the Son, and I first manifest it by all those texts above-mentioned, as also by these that follow: 2 Corinthians viii. 9, xiii. 14, Galatians vi. 18, Philippians iv. 23, 1 Thessalonians v. 28, 2 Thessalonians iii. 18, Philemon 25, Revelation xxii. 21. 3. It is also attributed to the Holy Ghost. Now, he is here called the Spirit of grace, because he is the author of grace as the Father, and the Son (Zech. xii. 10; Heb. x. 29).

So then, it remaineth that I show you, FIRST, How we are saved by the grace of the Father. SECOND, How we are saved by the grace of the Son. And, THIRD, How we are saved by the grace of the Spirit.

OF THE FATHER'S GRACE.

FIRST. How we are saved by the grace of the Father. Now this will I open unto you thus—

1. The Father by his grace hath bound up them that shall go to heaven in an eternal decree of election; and here, indeed, as was showed at first, is the beginning of our salvation (2 Tim. i. 9). And election is reckoned not the Son's act, but the Father's—'Blessed be the God and Father of our Lord Jesus Christ, who hath blessed us with all spiritual blessings in heavenly places in Christ, according as he hath chosen us in him before the foundation of the world' (Eph. i. 3, 4). Now this election is counted an act of grace—'So then, at this present time also, there is a remnant according to the election of grace' (Rom. xi. 5).

2. The Father's grace ordaineth and giveth the Son to undertake for us our redemption. The Father sent the Son to be the Saviour of the world—'In whom we have redemption through his blood, the forgiveness of sins, according to the riches of his grace; that in the ages to come he might shew the exceeding riches of his grace,

in his kindness toward us through Christ Jesus' (Eph. i. 7; ii. 7; 1 John iv. 14; John iii. 16; vi. 32, 33; xii. 49).

3. The Father's grace giveth us to Christ to be justified by his righteousness, washed in his blood, and saved by his life. This Christ mentioneth, and tells us it is his Father's will that they should be safe- coming at the last day, and that he had kept them all the days of his life, and they shall never perish (John vi. 37-39; xvii. 2, 12).

4. The Father's grace giveth the kingdom of heaven to those that he hath given to Jesus Christ—'Fear not, little flock, for it is your Father's good pleasure to give you the kingdom' (Luke xii. 32).

5. The Father's grace provideth and layeth up in Christ, for those that he hath chosen, a sufficiency of all spiritual blessings, to be communicated to them at their need, for their preservation in the faith, and faithful perseverance through this life; 'not according to our works, but according to his own purpose and grace, which was given us in Christ Jesus before the world began' (2 Tim. i. 9; Eph. i. 3, 4).

6. The Father's grace saveth us by the blessed and effectual call that he giveth us to the fellowship of his Son Jesus Christ (1 Col. i. 9; Gal. i. 15).

7. The Father's grace saveth us by multiplying pardons to us, for Christ's sake, day by day—'In whom we have redemption through his blood, the forgiveness of sins, according to the riches of his grace' (Eph. i. 7).

8. The Father's grace saves us by exercising patience and forbearance towards us all the time of our unregeneracy (Rom. iii. 24).

9. The Father's grace saveth us by holding of us fast in his hand, and by keeping of us from all the power of the enemy—'My Father,' said Christ, 'that gave them me, is greater than all, and no man is able to pluck them out of my Father's hand' (John x. 29).

10. What shall I say? The Father's grace saveth us by accepting of our persons and services, by lifting up the light of his countenance upon us, by manifesting of

his love unto us, and by sending of his angels to fetch us to himself, when we have finished our pilgrimage in this world.

OF THE GRACE OF THE SON.

SECOND. I come now to speak of the grace of the Son; for as the Father putteth forth his grace in the saving of the sinner, so doth the Son put forth his—'For ye know the grace of our Lord Jesus Christ, that, though he was rich, yet for your sakes he became poor, that ye through his poverty might be rich' (2 Cor. viii. 9).

Here you see also that the grace of our Lord Jesus Christ is brought in as a partner with the grace of his Father in the salvation of our souls. Now this is the grace of our Lord Jesus Christ; he was rich, but for our sakes he became poor, that we through his poverty might be made rich.

To inquire, then, into this grace, this condescending grace of Christ, and that by searching out how rich Jesus Christ was, and then how poor he made himself, that we through his poverty might have the riches of salvation.

First. How rich was Jesus Christ? To which I answer—1. Generally; 2. Particularly.

1. Generally. He was rich as the Father—'All things that the Father hath,' saith he, 'are mine.' Jesus Christ is the Lord of all, God over all, blessed for ever. 'He thought it not robbery to be equal with God,' being naturally and eternally God, as the Father, but of his Godhead he could not strip himself (John x. 30; xvi. 15; Acts x. 36; Phil. ii. 6; Rom. ix. 4, 5).

2. Particularly. Jesus Christ had glory with the Father; yea, a manifold glory with him, which he stripped himself of.

(1.) He had the glory of dominion, he was Lord of all the creatures; they were under him upon a double account—(a) as he was their Creator (Col. i. 16); (b) as he was made the heir of God (Heb. i. 2).

(2.) Therefore the glory of worship, reverence, and

fear from all creatures, was due unto him; the worship, obedience, subjection, and service of angels were due unto him; the fear, honour, and glory of kings, and princes, and judges of the earth were due unto him; the obedience of the sun, moon, stars, clouds, and all vapours, were due unto him; all dragons, deeps, fire, hail, snow, mountains and hills, beasts, cattle, creeping things, and flying fowls, the service of them all, and their worship, were due unto him (Psa. cxlviii.).

(3.) The glory of the heavens themselves was due unto him; in a word, heaven and earth were his.

(4.) But above all, the glory of communion with his Father was his; I say, the glory of that unspeakable communion that he had with the Father before his incarnation, which alone was worth ten thousand worlds, that was ever his.

(5.) But again; as Jesus Christ was possessed with this, so, besides, he was Lord of life; this glory also was Jesus Christ's: 'In him was life,' therefore he is called the Prince of it; because it was in him originally as in the Father (Acts iii. 15). He gave to all life and breath, and all things; angels, men, beasts, they had all their life from him.

(6.) Again, as he was Lord of glory, and Prince of life, so he was also Prince of peace, (Isa. ix. 6); and by him was maintained that harmony and goodly order which were among things in heaven and things on earth.

Take things briefly in these few particulars—(a.) The heavens were his, and he made them. (b.) Angels were his, and he made them. (c.) The earth was his, and he made it. (d.) Man was his, and he made him.

[Second. How poor he made himself.] Now this heaven he forsook for our sakes—'He came into the world to save sinners' (1 Tim. i. 15).

[1.] He was made lower than the angels, for the suffering of death (Heb. ii. 9). When he was born, he made himself, as he saith, a worm, or one of no reputation; he became the reproach and byword of the people; he was born in a stable, laid in a manger, earned his bread with his labour, being by trade a carpenter (Psa. xxii. 6; Phil. ii. 7; Luke ii. 7; Mark vi. 3). When he betook himself to his ministry, he lived upon the charity of the people; when other men went to their own houses, Jesus went to the Mount of Olives. Hark what himself saith for the clearing of this—'Foxes have holes, and birds of the air have nests, but the Son of man hath not where to lay his head.' He denied himself of this world's good (Luke viii. 2, 3; ix. 58; John vii. 35; viii. 1).

[2.] Again, as he was Prince of life, so he for our sakes laid down that also; for so stood the matter, that he or we must die; but the grace that was in his heart wrought with him to lay down his life: 'He gave his life a ransom for many.' He laid down his life that we might have life; he gave his flesh and blood for the life of the world; he laid down his life for his sheep.

[3.] Again; he was Prince of peace, but he forsook his peace also. (1.) He laid aside peace with the world, and chose upon that account to be a man of sorrows and acquainted with grief, and therefore was persecuted from his cradle to his cross, by kings, rulers, &c. (2.) He laid aside his peace with his Father, and made himself the object of his Father's curse, insomuch that the Lord smote, struck, and afflicted him; and, in conclusion, hid his face from him (as he expressed, with great crying) at the hour of his death.

[OBJECT.] But perhaps some may say, What need was there that Jesus Christ should do all this? Could not the grace of the Father save us without this condescension of the Son?

ANSW. As there is grace, so there is justice in God; and man having sinned, God concluded to save him in a way of righteousness; therefore it was absolutely necessary that Jesus Christ should put himself into our very condition, sin only excepted. 1. Now by sin we had lost the glory of God, therefore Jesus Christ lays aside the glory that he had with the Father (Rom. iii. 23; John xvii. 5). 2. Man by sin had shut himself out of an earthly paradise, and Jesus Christ will leave his heavenly paradise to save him (Gen. iii. 24; 1 Tim. i. 15; John vi. 38, 39). 3. Man by sin had made himself lighter than vanity, and this Lord God, Jesus Christ, made himself lower than the angels to redeem him (Isa. xl. 17; Heb. ii. 7). 4. Man by sin lost his right to the creatures, and Jesus Christ will deny himself of a whole world to save him (Luke ix. 58). 5. Man by sin had made himself subject to death; but Jesus Christ will lose his life to save him (Rom. vi. 23). 6. Man by sin had procured to himself the curse of God; but Jesus Christ will bear that curse in his own body to save him (Gal. iii. 13). 7. Man by sin had lost peace with God; but this would Jesus Christ lose also, to the end man might be saved. 8. Man should have been mocked of God, therefore Christ was mocked of men. 9. Man should have been scourged in hell; but, to hinder that, Jesus was scourged on earth. 10. Man should have been crowned with ignominy and shame; but, to prevent that, Jesus was crowned with thorns. 11. Man should have been pierced with the spear of God's wrath; but, to prevent that, Jesus was pierced both by God and men. 12. Man should have been rejected of God and angels; but, to prevent that, Jesus was forsaken of God, and denied, hated, and rejected of men (Isa. xlviii. 22; Prov. i. 24-26; Matt. xxvii. 26, 39, 46; Psa. ix. 17; xi. 6; xxii. 7; Dan. xii. 2; John xix. 2-5, 37; Num. xxiv. 8; Zech. xii. 10; Luke ix. 22).

I might thus enlarge, and that by authority from this text—'He became poor, that ye through his poverty might be rich.' All the riches he stripped himself of, it was for our sakes; all the sorrows he underwent, it was for our sakes; to the least circumstance of the sufferings of Christ there was necessity that so it should be, all was for our sakes: 'For our sakes he became poor, that ye through his poverty might be rich.'

And you see the argument that prevailed with Christ to do this great service for man, the grace that was in his heart; as also the prophet saith, 'In his love and in his pity he redeemed them.' According to this in the Corinthians, 'Ye know the grace of our Lord Jesus Christ'; both which agree with the text, 'By grace ye are saved.'

I say, this was the grace of the Son, and the exercise thereof. The Father therefore shows his grace one way, and the Son his another. It was not the Father, but the Son, that left his heaven for sinners; it was not the Father, but the Son, that spilt his blood for sinners. The Father indeed gave the Son, and blessed be the Father for that; and the Son gave his life and blood for us, and blessed be the Son for that.

But methinks we should not yet have done with this grace of the Son. Thou Son of the Blessed, what grace was manifest in thy condescension! Grace brought thee down from heaven, grace stripped thee of thy glory, grace made thee poor and despicable, grace made thee bear such burdens of sin, such burdens of sorrow, such burdens of God's curse as are unspeakable. O Son of God! grace was in all thy tears, grace came bubbling out of thy side with thy blood, grace came forth with every word of thy sweet mouth (Psa. xlv. 2; Luke iv. 22). Grace came out where the whip smote thee, where the thorns pricked thee, where the nails and spear pierced thee. O blessed Son of God! Here is grace indeed! Unsearchable riches of grace! Unthought-of riches of grace! Grace to make angels wonder, grace to make sinners happy, grace to astonish devils. And what will become of them that trample under foot this Son of God?

OF THE GRACE OF THE SPIRIT.

THIRD. I come now to speak of the grace of the Spirit; for he also saveth us by his grace. The Spirit, I told you, is God, as the Father and the Son, and is therefore also the author of grace; yea, and it is absolutely necessary that he put forth his grace also, or else no flesh can be saved. The Spirit of God hath his hand in saving of us many ways; for they that go to heaven, as they must be beholding to the Father and the Son, so also to the Spirit of God. The Father chooseth us, giveth us to Christ, and heaven to us, and the like. The Son fulfills the law for us, takes the curse of the law from us, bears in his own body our sorrows, and sets us justified in the sight of God. The Father's grace is showed in heaven and earth; the Son's grace is showed on the earth, and on the cross; and the Spirit's grace must be showed in our souls and bodies, before we come to heaven.

Quest. But some may say, Wherein doth the saving grace of the Spirit appear?

Answ. In many things.

In taking possession of us for his own, in his making of us his house and habitation, so that though the Father and the Son have both gloriously put forth gracious acts in order to our salvation, yet the Spirit is the first that makes seizure of us (1 Cor. iii. 16; vi. 19; Eph. ii. 21, 22). Christ, therefore, when he went away, said not that he would send the Father, but the Spirit, and that he should be in us for ever— 'If I depart,' said Christ, 'I will send him, the Spirit of truth, the Comforter' (John xiv. 16; xvi. 7, 13).

The Holy Spirit coming into us, and dwelling in us, worketh out many salvations for us now, and each of them in order also to our being saved for ever.

1. He saveth us from our darkness by illuminating of us; hence he is called 'the Spirit of revelation,' because he openeth the blind eyes, and so consequently delivereth us from that darkness which else would drown us in the deeps of hell (Eph. i. 17, 19).

2. He it is that convinceth us of the evil of our unbelief, and that shows us the necessity of our believing in Christ; without the conviction of this we should perish (John xvi. 9).

3. This is that finger of God by which the devil is made to give place unto grace, by whose power else we should be carried headlong to hell (Luke xi. 20-22).

4. This is he that worketh faith in our hearts, without which neither the grace of the Father nor the grace of the Son can save us, 'For he that believeth not, shall be damned' (Mark xvi. 16; Rom. xv. 13).

5. This is he by whom we are born again; and he that is not so born can neither see nor inherit the kingdom of heaven (John iii. 3-7).

6. This is he that setteth up his kingdom in the heart, and by that means keepeth out the devil after he is cast out, which kingdom of the Spirit, whoever wanteth, they lie liable to a worse possession of the devil than ever (Matt. xii. 43-45; Luke xi. 24, 25).

7. By this Spirit we come to see the beauty of Christ, without a sight of which we should never desire him, but should certainly live in the neglect of him, and perish (John xvi. 14; 1 Cor. ii. 9-13; Isa. liii. 1, 2).

8. By this Spirit we are helped to praise God acceptably, but without it, it is impossible to be heard unto salvation (Rom. viii. 26; Eph. vi. 18; 1 Cor. xiv. 15).

9. By this blessed Spirit the love of God is shed abroad in our hearts, and our hearts are directed into the love of God (Rom. v. 5; 2 Thess. ii. 13).

10. By this blessed Spirit we are led from the ways of the flesh into the ways of life, and by it our mortal body, as well as our immortal soul, is quickened in the service of God (Gal. v. 18, 25; Rom. viii. 11).

11. By this good Spirit we keep that good thing, even the seed of God, that at the first by the Word of God was infused into us, and without which we are liable to the worst damnation (1 John iii. 9; 1 Peter i. 23; 2 Tim. i. 14).

12. By this good Spirit we have help and light against all the wisdom and cunning of the world, which putteth forth itself in its most cursed sophistications to overthrow the simplicity that is in Christ (Matt. x. 19, 20; Mark xiii. 11; Luke xii. 11, 12).

13. By this good Spirit our graces are maintained in life and vigour, as faith, hope, love, a spirit of prayer, and every grace (2 Cor. iv. 13; Rom. xv. 13; 2 Tim. i. 7; Eph. vi. 18; Titus iii. 5).

14. By this good Spirit we are sealed to the day of redemption (Eph. i. 14).

15. And by this good Spirit we are made to wait

with patience until the redemption of the purchased possession comes (Gal. v. 5).

Now all these things are so necessary to our salvation, that I know not which of them can be wanting; neither can any of them be by any means attained but by this blessed Spirit.

And thus have I in few words showed you the grace of the Spirit, and how it putteth forth itself towards the saving of the soul. And verily, Sirs, it is necessary that you know these things distinctly—to wit, the grace of the Father, the grace of the Son, and the grace of the Holy Ghost; for it is not the grace of one, but of all these three, that saveth him that shall be saved indeed.

The Father's grace saveth no man without the grace of the Son; neither doth the Father and the Son save any without the grace of the Spirit; for as the Father loves, the Son must die, and the Spirit must sanctify, or no soul must be saved.

Some think that the love of the Father, without the blood of the Son, will save them, but they are deceived; for 'without shedding of blood is no remission' (Heb. ix. 22).

Some think that the love of the Father and blood of the Son will do, without the holiness of the Spirit of God; but they are deceived also; for 'if any man have not the Spirit of Christ, he is none of his'; and again, 'without holiness no man shall see the Lord' (Rom. viii. 9; Heb. xii. 14).

There is a third sort, that think the holiness of the Spirit is sufficient of itself; but they (if they had it) are deceived also; for it must be the grace of the Father, the grace of the Son, and the grace of the Spirit, jointly, that must save them.

But yet, as these three do put forth grace jointly and truly in the salvation of a sinner, so they put it forth, as I also have showed you before, after a diverse manner. The Father designs us for heaven, the Son redeems from sin and death, and the Spirit makes us meet for heaven; not by electing, that is the work of the Father; not by dying, that is the work of the Son; but by his revealing Christ, and applying Christ to our souls, by shedding the love of God abroad in our hearts, by sanctifying of our souls, and taking possession of us as an earnest of our possession of heaven.

QUESTION III.

WHO ARE THEY THAT ARE TO BE SAVED BY GRACE?

I come now to the third particular—namely, to show you who they are that are to be saved by grace.

[Who are not saved.] First. Not the self-righteous, not they that have no need of the physician. 'The whole have no need of the physician,' saith Christ. 'I came not to call the righteous, but sinners to repentance' (Mark ii. 17). And again, 'He hath filled the hungry with good things, and the rich he hath sent empty away' (Luke i. 53). Now when I say not the self- righteous nor the rich, I mean not that they are utterly excluded; for Paul was such an one; but he saveth not such without he first awaken them to see they have need to be saved by grace.

Second. The grace of God saveth not him that hath sinned the unpardonable sin. There is nothing left for him 'but a certain fearful looking for of judgment, - which shall devour the adversaries' (Heb. x. 26, 27).

Third. That sinner that persevereth in final impenitency and unbelief shall be damned (Luke xiii. 3, 5; Rom. ii. 2-5; Mark xvi. 15, 16).

Fourth. That sinner whose mind the god of this world hath blinded, that the glorious light of the gospel of Christ, who is the image of God, can never shine into him, is lost, and must be damned (2 Cor. iv. 3, 4).

Fifth. The sinner that maketh religion his cloak for

wickedness, he is a hypocrite, and, continuing so, must certainly be damned (Psa. cxxv. 5; Isa. xxxiii. 14; Matt. xxiv. 50, 51).

Sixth. In a word, every sinner that persevereth in his wickedness, shall not inherit the kingdom of heaven—'Know ye not that the unrighteous shall not inherit the kingdom of God? Be not deceived: neither fornicators, nor idolaters, nor adulterers, nor effeminate, nor abusers of themselves with mankind, nor thieves, nor covetous, nor drunkards, nor revilers, nor extortioners, shall inherit the kingdom of God.' 'Let no man deceive you with vain words; for because of these things cometh the wrath of God upon the children of disobedience' (1 Cor. vi. 9-12; Eph. v. 5, 6).

[Who are saved.] QUESTION. But what kind of sinners shall then be saved?

ANSW. Those of all these kinds that the Spirit of God shall bring [to] the Father by Jesus Christ; these, I say, and none but these, can be saved, because else the sinners might be saved without the Father, or without the Son, or without the Spirit.

Now, in all that I have said, I have not in the least suggested that any sinner is rejected because his sins, in the nature of them, are great; Christ Jesus came into the world to save the chief of sinners. It is not, therefore, the greatness of, but the continuance in, sins that indeed damneth the sinner. But I always exclude him that hath sinned against the Holy Ghost. That it is not the greatness of sin that excludeth the sinner is evident—

1. From the words before the text, which doth give an account of what kind of sinners were here saved by grace, as namely, they that were dead in trespasses and sins, those that walked in these sins, 'according to the course of this world, according to the prince of the power of the air, the spirit that now worketh in the children of disobedience: among whom also we all had our conversation in times past in the lusts of our flesh, fulfilling the desires of the flesh and of the mind; and were by nature the children of wrath, even as others'

(Eph. ii. 2, 3).

2. It is evident also from the many sinners that we find to be saved, by the revealed will of God. For in the Word we have mention made of the salvation of great sinners, where their names and their sins stand recorded for our encouragement; as, (1.) You read of Manasseh, who was an idolater, a witch, a persecutor, yea, a rebel against the word of God, sent unto him by the prophets; and yet this man was saved (2 Chron. xxxiii. 2-13; 2 Kings xxi. 16). (2.) You read of Mary Magdalene, in whom were seven devils; her condition was dreadful, yet she was saved (Luke viii. 2; John xx.). (3.) You read of the man that had a legion of devils in him. O how dreadful was his condition! and yet by grace he was saved (Mark v. 1-10). (4.) You read of them that murdered the Lord Jesus, and how they were converted and saved (Acts ii. 23). (5.) You read of the exorcists, how they closed with Christ, and were saved by grace (Acts xix. 13). (6.) You read of Saul the persecutor, and how he was saved by grace (Acts ix. 15).

OBJECT. But, thou sayest, I am a backslider.

ANSW. So was Noah, and yet he found grace in the eyes of the Lord (Gen. ix. 21, 22). So was Lot, and yet God saved him by grace (Gen. xix. 35; 2 Peter ii. 7-9). So was David, yet by grace he was forgiven his iniquities (2 Sam. xii. 7-13). So was Solomon, and a great one too; yet by grace his soul was saved (Psa. lxxxix. 28-34). So was Peter, and that a dreadful one; yet by grace he was saved (Matt. xxvi. 69-74; Mark xvi. 7; Acts xv. 7-11). Besides, for further encouragement, read Jeremiah iii., xxxiii. 25, 26, li. 5, Ezekiel xxxvi. 25, Hosea xiv. 1-4; and stay thyself, and wonder at the riches of the grace of God.

QUEST. But how should we find out what sinners shall be saved? All, it seems, shall not. Besides, for aught can be gathered by what you have said, there is as bad saved as damned, set him that hath sinned the unpardonable sin aside.

ANSW. True, there are as bad saved as damned;

QUESTION III.

but to this question: They that are effectually called, are saved. They that believe on the Son of God shall be saved. They that are sanctified and preserved in Christ shall be saved. They that take up their cross daily, and follow Christ, shall be saved.

Take a catalogue of them thus: 'Believe on the Lord Jesus Christ, and thou shalt be saved' (Mark xvi. 16; Acts xvi. 31). 'If thou shalt confess with thy mouth the Lord Jesus, and shalt believe in thine heart that God hath raised him from the dead thou shalt be saved' (Rom. x. 9). Be justified by the blood of Christ, and thou shalt be saved (Rom. v. 9). Be reconciled to God by the death of his Son, and thou shalt be saved by his life (Rom. v. 10). 'And it shall come to pass, that whosoever shall call on the name of the Lord shall be saved' (Acts ii. 21).

See some other scriptures. 'He shall save the humble person' (Job xxii. 29). 'Thou wilt save the afflicted people' (Psa. xviii. 27). 'He shall save the children of the needy' (Psa. lxxii. 4). 'He shall save the souls of the needy' (Psa. lxxii. 13). 'O thou, my God, save thy servant that trusteth in thee' (Psa. lxxxvi. 2). 'He will fulfill the desire of them that fear him, he also will hear their cry, and will save them' (Psa. cxlv. 19).

[Caution.] But, sinner, if thou wouldst indeed be saved, beware of these four things—

1. Beware of delaying repentance; delays are dangerous and damnable; they are dangerous, because they harden the heart; they are damnable, because their tendency is to make thee outstand the time of grace (Psa. xcv. 7; Heb. iii.-xii.).

2. Beware of resting in the word of the kingdom, without the spirit and power of the kingdom of the gospel; for the gospel coming in word only saves nobody, for the kingdom of God or the gospel, where it comes to salvation, is not in word but in power (1 Thess. i. 4-6; 1 Cor. iv. 19).

3. Take heed of living in a profession, a life that is provoking to God; for that is the way to make him cast thee away in his anger.

4. Take heed that thy inside and outside be alike;, and both conformable to the Word of his grace; labour to be like the living creatures which thou mayest read of in the book of the prophet Ezekiel, whose appearance and themselves were one[10] (Ezek. x. 22).

In all this, I have advertised you not to be content without the power and Spirit of God in your hearts, for without him you partake of none of the grace of the Father or Son, but will certainly miss of the salvation of the soul.

---

10 'Their appearance and themselves'; this beautiful illustration might escape the reader's notice, unless specially directed to it. The living creatures were always the same, although seen under different circumstances, and in diverse places. Inside and out they were the same; without deviation or turning, they went straight forward. It is well said that Bunyan has here snatched a grace beyond the reach of art, and has applied it to exalt and beautify consistency of Christian character.—ED.

QUESTION IV.

HOW IT APPEARS THAT THEY THAT ARE SAVED, ARE SAVED BY GRACE?

This fourth question requireth that some demonstration be given of the truth of this doctrine—to wit, that they that are saved are saved by grace.

What hath been said before hath given some demonstration of the truth; wherefore, first repeating in few words the sum of what hath been said already, I shall come to further proof. 1. That this is true, the Scriptures testify, because God chose them to salvation before they had done good (Rom. ix. 11). 2. Christ was ordained to be their Saviour before the foundation of the world (Eph. i. 4; 1 Peter i. 19-21). 3. All things that concur and go to our salvation were also in the same laid up in Christ, to be communicated in the dispensation of the fullness of times, to them that shall be saved (Eph. i. 3, 4; 2 Tim. i. 9; Eph. i. 10; iii. 8-11; Rom. viii. 30).

[That salvation is by grace appears in its contrivance.] Again, as their salvation was contrived by God, so, as was said, this salvation was undertaken by one of the three; to wit, the Son of the Father (John i. 29; Isa. xlviii. 16).

Had there been a contrivance in heaven about the salvation of sinners on earth, yet if the result of that contrivance had been that we should be saved by our own good deeds, it would not have been proper for an apostle, or an angel, to say, 'By grace ye are saved.' But now, when a council is held in eternity about the salvation of sinners in time, and when the result of that council shall be, that the Father, the Son, and the Holy Ghost will themselves accomplish the work of this salvation, this is grace, this is naturally grace, grace that is rich and free; yea, this is unthought-of grace. I will say it again, this is unthought-of grace; for who could have thought that a Saviour had been in the bosom of the Father, or that the Father would have given him to be the Saviour of men, since he refused to give him to be the Saviour of angels? (Heb. ii. 16, 17).

[Grace appears in the Son's undertaking this work.] Again; could it have been thought that the Father would have sent his Son to be the Saviour, we should, in reason, have thought also that he would never have taken the work wholly upon himself, especially that fearful, dreadful, soul-astonishing, and amazing part thereof! Who could once have imagined that the Lord Jesus would have made himself so poor as to stand before God in the nauseous rags of our sins, and subject himself to the curse and death that were due to our sin? but thus he did to save us by grace.

'Blessed be the God and Father of our Lord Jesus Christ, who hath blessed us with all spiritual blessings in heavenly places in Christ: according as he hath chosen us in him before the foundation of the world, that we should be holy and without blame before him in love: having predestinated us unto the adoption of children by Jesus Christ to himself, according to the good pleasure of his will, to the praise of the glory of his grace, wherein he hath made us accepted in the Beloved; in whom we have redemption through his blood, the forgiveness of sins, according to the riches of his grace' (Eph. i. 3-7).

[Grace appears in the terms and conditions on which salvation is made over.] Again; if we consider the terms and conditions upon which this salvation is made over to them that are saved, it will further appear we are saved by grace.

1. The things that immediately concern our justification and salvation, they are offered, yea, given to us freely, and we are commanded to receive them by faith. Sinner, hold up thy lap. God so loved the world, that he giveth his Son, that he giveth his righteousness, that he giveth his Spirit, and the kingdom of heaven (John iii. 16; Rom. v. 17; 2 Cor. i. 21, 22; Luke xii. 32).

2. He also giveth repentance, he giveth faith, and giveth everlasting consolation, and good hope through grace (Acts v. 30, 31; Phil. i. 29; 2 Thess. ii. 16).

3. He giveth pardon, and giveth more grace, to keep us from sinking into hell, than we have sin to sink us in thither (Acts v. 31; Prov. iii. 34; John iv. 6; 1 Peter v. 5).

4. He hath made all these things over to us in a covenant of grace. We call it a covenant of grace, because it is set in opposition to the covenant of works, and because it is established to us in the doings of Christ, founded in his blood, established upon the best promises made to him, and to us by him. 'For all the promises of God in him are yea, and in him amen, to the glory of God by us' (2 Cor. i. 20).

But to pass these, and to come to some other demonstrations for the clearing of this—

Let us a little consider,

What man is, upon whom the Father, the Son, and the Spirit bestows this grace.

1. [An enemy to God.] By nature he is an enemy to God, an enemy in his mind. 'The carnal mind is enmity against God, for it is not subject to the law of God, neither indeed can be' (Rom. viii. 7; Col. i. 21).

2. [A slave to sin.] So that the state of man was this—he was not only over persuaded on a sudden to sin against God, but he drank this sin, like water, into his very nature, mingled it with every faculty of his soul and member of his body; by the means of which he became alienated from God, and an enemy to him in his

very heart; and wilt thou, O Lord, as the Scripture hath it, 'And dost thou open thine eyes upon such an one?' (Job xiv. 3). Yea, open thy heart, and take this man, not into judgment, but into mercy with thee?

3. [In covenant with death and hell.] Further, man by his sin had not only given himself to be a captive slave to the devil, but, continuing in his sin, he made head against his God, struck up a covenant with death, and made an agreement with hell; but for God to open his eyes upon such an one, and to take hold of him by riches of grace, this is amazing (Isa. xxviii. 16-18).

See where God found the Jew when he came to look upon him to save him—'As for thy nativity,' says God, 'in the day thou wast born thy navel was not cut, neither wast thou washed in water to supple thee; thou wast not salted at all, nor swaddled at all. None eye pitied thee, to do any of these unto thee, to have compassion upon thee; but thou wast cast out in the open field, to the loathing of thy person, in the day that thou wast born. And when I passed by thee, and saw thee polluted in thine own blood, I said unto thee, when thou wast in thy blood, Live; yea, I said unto thee, when thou wast in thy blood, Live. - Now when I passed by thee, and looked upon thee, behold, thy time was the time of love; and I spread my skirt over thee, and covered thy nakedness; yea, I sware unto thee, and entered into a covenant with thee, saith the Lord God, and thou becamest mine.' Sinner, see further into the chapter, Ezekiel xvi. All this is the grace of God; every word in this text smells of grace.

But before I pass this, let us a little take notice of

THE CARRIAGE OF GOD TO MAN, AND AGAIN OF MAN TO GOD, IN HIS CONVERSION.

FIRST. OF GOD'S CARRIAGE TO MAN. He comes to him while he is in his sins, in his blood; he comes to him now, not in the heat and fire of his jealousy, but 'in the cool of the day,' in unspeakable gentleness, mercy, pity, and bowels of love; not in clothing himself with vengeance, but in a way of entreaty, and meekly beseecheth the sinner to be reconciled unto him (2 Cor. v. 19, 20).

It is expected among men that he which giveth the offence should be the first in seeking peace; but, sinner, betwixt God and man it is not so; not that we loved God, not that we chose God; but 'God was in Christ, reconciling the world unto himself, not imputing their trespasses unto them.' God is the first that seeketh peace; and, as I said, in a way of entreaty he bids his ministers pray you in Christ's stead; 'as though God did beseech you by us, we pray you, in Christ's stead, be ye reconciled to God.' O sinner, wilt thou not open? Behold, God the Father and his Son Jesus Christ stand both at the door of thy heart, beseeching there for favour from thee, that thou wilt be reconciled to them, with promise, if thou wilt comply, to forgive thee all thy sins. O grace! O amazing grace! To see a prince entreat a beggar to receive an alms would be a strange sight; to see a king entreat the traitor to accept of mercy would be a stranger sight than that; but to see God entreat a sinner, to hear Christ say, 'I stand at the door and knock,' with a heart full and a heaven full of grace to bestow upon him that opens, this is such a sight as dazzles the eyes of angels. What sayest thou now, sinner? Is not this God rich in mercy? Hath not this God great love for sinners? Nay, further, that thou mayest not have any ground to doubt that all this is but complementing, thou hast also here declared that God hath made his Christ 'to be sin for us, who knew no sin, that we might be made the righteousness of God in him.' If God would have stuck at anything, he would have stuck at the death of his Son; but he 'delivered him up for us' freely; 'how shall he not with him also freely give us all things?' (Rom. viii. 32).[11]

---

11 This is one of Bunyan's peculiarly affecting representations, which in preaching went to the heart, producing intense interest, and tears of contrition over the stubbornness of human nature. Reader, Bunyan, being dead, yet speaketh; can you feel unaffected under such an appeal?—ED.

But this is not all. God doth not only beseech thee to be reconciled to him, but further, for thy encouragement, he hath pronounced, in thy hearing, exceeding great and precious promises; 'and hath confirmed it by an oath, that by two immutable things, in which it was impossible for God to lie, we might have a strong consolation, who have fled for refuge to lay hold upon the hope set before us' (Heb. vi. 18, 19; Isa. i. 18; lv. 6, 7; Jer. li. 5).

SECOND. OF MAN'S CARRIAGE TO GOD. Let us come now to the carriage of these sinners to God, and that from the first day he beginneth to deal with their souls, even to the time that they are to be taken up into heaven. And,

First. To begin with God's ordinary dealing with sinners, when at first he ministereth conviction to them by his Word, how strangely do they behave themselves! They love not to have their consciences touched; they like not to ponder upon what they have been, what they are, or what is like to become of them hereafter; such thoughts they count unmanly, hurtful, disadvantageous; therefore 'they refused to hearken, and pulled away the shoulder, and stopped their ears, that they should not hear' (Zech. vii. 11). And now they are for anything rather than the Word; an alehouse, a whorehouse, a playhouse, sports, pleasures, sleep, the world, and what not so they may stave[12] off the power of the word of God.

Second. If God now comes up closer to them, and begins to fasten conviction upon the conscience, though such conviction be the first step to faith and repentance, yea, and to life eternal, yet what shifts will they have to forget them, and wear them off! Yea, although they now begin to see that they must either turn or burn,[13] yet

---

12 'To stave,' to thrust, to push, to delay.—ED.

13 These terms are taken from Foxe's Martyrology. It was frequently the brutal remark of the Judges, You must turn or burn. Bunyan here applies it to turning from sin or burning in hell.—ED.

QUESTION IV.

oftentimes even then they will study to wave a present conversion: they object, they are too young to turn yet; seven years hence time enough, when they are old, or come upon a sick-bed. O what an enemy is man to his own salvation! I am persuaded that God hath visited some of you often with his Word, even twice and thrice, and you have thrown water as fast as he hath by the Word cast fire upon your conscience.[14]

Christian, what had become of thee if God had taken thy denial for an answer, and said, Then will I carry the word of salvation to another, and he will hear it? Sinner, turn, says God. Lord, I cannot tend[15] it, says the sinner. Turn or burn, says God. I will venture that, says the sinner. Turn, and be saved, says God. I cannot leave my pleasures, says the sinner: sweet sins, sweet pleasures, sweet delights, says the sinner. But what grace is it in God thus to parley with the sinner! O the patience of God to a poor sinner! What if God should now say, Then get thee to thy sins, get thee to thy delights, get thee to thy pleasures, take them for thy portion, they shall be all thy heaven, all thy happiness, and all thy portion?

Third. But God comes again, and shows the sinner the necessity of turning now; now or not at all; yea, and giveth the sinner this conviction so strongly, that he cannot put it off. But behold, the sinner has one spark of enmity still. If he must needs turn now, he will either turn from one sin to another, from great ones to little ones, from many to few, or from all to one, and there stop. But perhaps convictions will not thus leave him. Why, then, he will turn from profaneness to the law of Moses, and will dwell as long as God will let him upon his own seeming goodness. And now observe him, he

---

14 This treatise having been written some years after the Pilgrim's Progress, Bunyan very naturally refers to the well-known scene in the Interpreter's House, where the fire is kept burning by oil from behind the wall, in spite of all the water thrown upon its flames.—ED.

15 'To tend,' to watch, to guard, to attend.—ED.

is a great stickler for legal performance; now he will be a good neighbour, he will pay every man his own, will leave off his swearing, the alehouse, his sports, and carnal delights; he will read, pray, talk of Scripture, and be a very busy one in religion, such as it is; now he will please God, and make him amends for all the wrong he hath done him, and will feed him with chapters, and prayers, and promises, and vows, and a great many more such dainty dishes as these, persuading himself that now he must needs be fair for heaven, and thinks besides that he serveth God as well as any man in England can.[16]

But all this while he is as ignorant of Christ as the stool he sits on, and no nearer heaven than was the blind Pharisee; only he has got in a cleaner way to hell than the rest of his neighbours are in—'There is a generation that are pure in their own eyes, and yet is not washed from their filthiness' (Prov. xxx. 12).

Might not God now cut off this sinner, and cast him out of his sight; might he not leave him here to his own choice, to be deluded by, and to fall in his own righteousness, because he 'trusteth to it, and commits iniquity'? (Ezek. xxxiii. 13). But grace, preventing grace, preserves him. It is true, this turn of the sinner, as I said, is a turning short of Christ; but,

Fourth. God in this way of the sinner will mercifully follow him, and show him the shortness of his performances, the emptiness of his duties, and the uncleanness of his righteousness (Isa. xxviii. 20; lxiv. 6). Thus I speak of the sinner, the salvation of whose soul is graciously intended and contrived of God; for he shall by gospel light be wearied out of all; he shall be made to see the vanity of all, and that the personal righteousness of Jesus Christ, and that only, is it which of God is ordained to save the sinner from the due re-

---

16 How pointedly, how admirably, does this illustrate the fond absurdities, the extreme follies of the human heart! 'To serve God with such dainty dishes,' the cleanest being befouled with sin. 'A cleaner way to hell than our neighbours!'—ED.

ward of his sins. But behold, the sinner now, at the sight and sense of his own nothingness, falleth into a kind of despair; for although he hath it in him to presume of salvation, through the delusiveness of his own good opinion of himself, yet he hath it not in himself to have a good opinion of the grace of God in the righteousness of Christ; wherefore he concludeth, that if salvation be alone of the grace of God, through the righteousness of Christ, and that all of a man's own is utterly rejected, as to the justification of his person with God, then he is cast away. Now the reason of this sinking of heart is the sight that God hath given him, a sight of the uncleanness of his best performance; the former sight of his immoralities did somewhat distress him, and make him betake himself to his own good deeds to ease his conscience, wherefore this was his prop, his stay; but behold, now God hath taken this from under him, and now he falls; wherefore his best doth also now forsake him, and flies away like the morning dew, or a bird, or as the chaff that is driven with the whirlwind, and the smoke out of a chimney (Hosea ix. 11; xiii. 3). Besides, this revelation of the emptiness of his own righteousness, brings also with it a further discovery of the naughtiness of his heart, in its hypocrisies, pride, unbelief, hardness of heart, deadness, and backwardness to all gospel and new-covenant obedience, which sight of himself lies like millstones upon his shoulders, and sinks him yet further into doubts and fears of damnation. For, bid him now receive Christ, he answers he cannot, he dares not. Ask him why he cannot, he will answer he has no faith, nor hope in his heart. Tell him that grace is offered him freely, he says, but I have no heart to receive it; besides, he finds not, as he thinks, any gracious disposition in his soul, and therefore concludes he doth not belong to God's mercy, nor hath an interest in the blood of Christ, and therefore dares not presume to believe; wherefore, as I said, he sinks in his heart, he dies in his thoughts, he doubts, he despairs, and concludes he shall never be saved.

Fifth. But behold, the God of all grace leaveth him not in this distress, but comes up now to him closer than ever; he sends the Spirit of adoption, the blessed Comforter, to him, to tell him, 'God is love,' and therefore not willing to reject the broken in heart; bids him cry and pray for an evidence of mercy to his soul, and says, 'Peradventure you may be hid in the day of the Lord's anger.' At this the sinner takes some encouragement, yet he can get no more than that which will hang upon a mere probability, which by the next doubt that ariseth in the heart is blown quite away, and the soul left again in his first plight, or worse, where he lamentably bewails his miserable state, and is tormented with a thousand fears of perishing, for he hears not a word from heaven, perhaps for several weeks together. Wherefore unbelief begins to get the mastery of him, and takes off the very edge and spirit of prayer, and inclination to hear the Word any longer; yea, the devil also claps in with these thoughts, saying that all your prayers, and hearing, and reading, and godly company which you frequent, will rise up in judgment against you at last; therefore better it is, if you must be damned, to choose as easy a place in hell as you can. The soul at this, being quite discouraged, thinks to do as it hath been taught, and with dying thoughts it begins to faint when it goeth to prayer or to hear the word; but behold, when all hope seems to be quite gone, and the soul concludes, I DIE, I PERISH, in comes, on a sudden, the Spirit of God again, with some good word of God, which the soul never thought of before, which word of God commands a calm in the soul, makes unbelief give place, encourageth to hope and wait upon God again; perhaps it gives some little sight of Christ to the soul, and of his blessed undertaking for sinners. But behold, so soon as the power of things does again begin to wear off the heart, the sinner gives place to unbelief, questions God's mercy, and fears damning again; he also entertains hard thoughts of God and Christ, and thinks former encouragements were fancies, delusions, or

QUESTION IV.

mere think-so's. And why doth not God now cast the sinner to hell for his thus abusing his mercy and grace. O no! 'He will have mercy on whom he will have mercy, and he will have compassion on whom he will have compassion'; wherefore 'goodness and mercy shall follow him all the days of his life, that he may dwell in the house of the Lord for ever' (Psa. xxiii. 6).

Sixth. God, therefore, after all these provocations, comes by his Spirit to the soul again, and brings sealing grace and pardon to the conscience, testifying to it that its sins are forgiven, and that freely, for the sake of the blood of Christ; and now has the sinner such a sight of the grace of God in Christ as kindly breaks his heart with joy and comfort; now the soul knows what it is to eat promises; it also knows what it is to eat and drink the flesh and blood of Jesus Christ by faith; now it is driven by the power of his grace to its knees, to thank God for forgiveness of sins and for hopes of an inheritance amongst them that are sanctified by faith which is in Christ; now it hath a calm and sunshine; now 'he washeth his steps with butter, and the rock pours him out rivers of oil' (Job xxix. 6).

Seventh. But after this, perhaps the soul grows cold again, it also forgets this grace received, and waxeth carnal, begins again to itch after the world, loseth the life and savour of heavenly things, grieves the Spirit of God, woefully backslides, casteth off closet duties quite, or else retains only the formality of them, is a reproach to religion, grieves the hearts of them that are awake, and tender of God's name, &c. But what will God do now? Will he take this advantage to destroy the sinner? No. Will he let him alone in his apostasy? No. Will he leave him to recover himself by the strength of his now languishing graces? No. What then? Why, he will seek this man out till he finds him, and bring him home to himself again: 'For thus saith the Lord God, Behold, I, even I, will both search my sheep, and seek them out. As a shepherd seeketh out his flock in the day that he is among the sheep that are scattered; so will I seek out my sheep, and will deliver them out of all places where they have been scattered. - I will seek that which was lost, and bring again that which was driven away, and will bind up that which was broken, and will strengthen that which was sick' (Ezek. xxxiv. 11, 16).

Thus he dealt with the man that went down from Jerusalem to Jericho, and fell among thieves; and thus he dealt with the prodigal you read of also (Luke x. 30-35; xv. 20).

Of God's ordinary way of fetching the backslider home I will not now discourse—namely, whether he always breaketh his bones for his sins, as he broke David's; or whether he will all the days of their life, for this, leave them under guilt and darkness; or whether he will kill them now, that they may not be damned in the day of judgment, as he dealt with them at Corinth (1 Cor. xi. 30-32). He is wise, and can tell how to embitter backsliding to them he loveth. He can break their bones, and save them; he can lay them in the lowest pit, in darkness, in the deep, and save them; he can slay them as to this life, and save them. And herein again appears wonderful grace, that 'Israel is not forsaken, nor Judah of his God, though their land was filled with sin against the Holy One of Israel' (Jer. li. 5).

Eighth. But suppose God deals not either of these ways with the backslider, but shines upon him again, and seals up to him the remission of his sins a second time, saying, 'I will heal their backslidings, and love them freely,' what will the soul do now? Surely it will walk humbly now, and holily all its days. It will never backslide again, will it? It may happen it will not, it may happen it will; it is just as his God keeps him; for although his sins are of himself, his standing is of God; I say, his standing, while he stands, and his recovery, if he falls, are both of God; wherefore, if God leaves him a little, the next gap he finds, away he is gone again. 'My people,' says God, 'are bent to backsliding from me.' How many times did David backslide; yea, Jehoshaphat and Peter! (2 Sam. xi., xxiv.; 2 Chron. xix. 1-3; xx. 1-5;

Matt. xxvi. 69-71; Gal. ii. 11-13). As also in the third of Jeremiah it is said, 'But thou hast played the harlot with many lovers, yet return unto me, saith the Lord' (verse 1). Here is grace! So many time as the soul backslides, so many times God brings him again—I mean, the soul that must be saved by grace—he renews his pardons, and multiplies them. 'Lo, all these things worketh God oftentimes with man' (Job xxxiii. 29).

Ninth. But see yet more grace. I will speak here of heart- wanderings, and of daily miscarriages—I mean, of these common infirmities that are incident to the best of saints, and that attend them in their best performances; not that I intend, for I cannot, mention them particularly, that would be a task impossible; but such there are, worldly thoughts, unclean thoughts, too low thoughts of God, of Christ, of the Spirit, words, ways, and ordinances of God, by which a Christian transgresses many times; may I not say, sometimes many hundred times a day; yea, for aught I know, there are some saints, and them not long-lived either, that must receive, before they enter into life, millions of pardons from God for these; and every pardon is an act of grace, through the redemption that is in Christ's blood.[17]

Seventy times seven times a day we sometimes sin against our brother; but how many times, in that day, do we sin against God? Lord, 'who can understand his errors? cleanse thou me from secret faults' [sins], said David. And again, 'If thou, Lord, shouldest mark iniquities, O Lord, who shall stand? But there is forgiveness with thee that thou mayest be feared' (Matt. xviii. 21, 22; Psa. xix. 12; cxxx. 3, 4).

But to mention some of them. Sometimes they question the very being of God, or foolishly ask how he came to be at first; sometimes they question the truth of his Word, and suspect the harmony thereof,

---

17 O how humbling a consideration! Our sins are numberless, of omission, of commission, openly and secretly; nay, in a thousand cases they escape the sinner's observation. 'Cleanse thou me from secret faults.'—ED.

because their blind hearts and dull heads cannot reconcile it; yea, all fundamental truths lie open sometimes to the censure of their unbelief and atheism; as, namely, whether there be such an one as Christ, such a thing as the day of judgment, or whether there will be a heaven or hell hereafter, and God pardons all these by his grace. When they believe these things, even then they sin, by not having such reverent, high, and holy thoughts of them as they ought; they sin also by having too, too good thoughts of themselves, of sin, and the world; sometimes, let me say, often, they wink too much at known sin, they bewail not, as they should, the infirmities of the flesh; the itching inclinations which they find in their hearts after vanity go too often from them unrepented of. I do not say but they repent them in the general. But all these things, O how often doth God forgive, through the riches of his grace!

They sin by not walking answerably to mercies received; yea, they come short in their thanks to God for them, even then when they most heartily acknowledge how unworthy they are of them; also, how little of the strength of them is spent to his praise, who freely poureth them into their bosoms; but from all these sins are they saved by grace. They sin in their most exact and spiritual performance of duties; they pray not, they hear not, they read not, they give not alms, they come not to the Lord's table, or other holy appointments of God, but in and with much coldness, deadness, wanderings of heart, ignorance, misapprehensions, &c. They forget God while they pray unto him; they forget Christ while they are at his table; they forget his Word even while they are reading of it.

How often do they make promises to God, and afterwards break them! Yea, or if they keep promise in show, how much doth their heart even grudge the performing of them; how do they shuck[18] at the cross; and how unwilling are they to lose that little they have for God, though all they have was given them to glorify

---

18 'Shuck,' to shake or start back.—Ed.

him withal![19]

All these things, and a thousand times as many more, dwell in the flesh of man; and they may as soon go away from themselves as from these corruptions; yea, they may sooner cut the flesh from their bones than these motions of sin from their flesh; these will be with them in every duty—I mean, some or other of them; yea, as often as they look, or think, or hear, or speak. These are with them, especially when the man intends good in so doing: 'When I would do good,' says Paul, 'evil is present with me.' And God himself complains that 'every imagination of the thoughts of the heart of man is only evil,' and that 'continually' (Rom. vii. 21; Gen. vi. 5).

By these things, therefore, we continually defile ourselves, and every one of our performances—I mean, in the judgment of the law—even mixing iniquity with those things which we hallow unto the Lord. 'For from within, out of the heart of men, proceed evil thoughts, adulteries, fornications, murders, thefts, covetousness, wickedness, deceit, lasciviousness, an evil eye, blasphemy, pride, foolishness; all these evil things come from within, and defile the man' (Mark vii. 21-23). Now what can deliver the soul from these but grace? 'By grace ye are saved.'

---

19 In Bunyan's time, the saints of God were sorely tormented by penalties, fines, and imprisonments. It required great faith in a mother, who saw all her goods seized, for not going to church, the incarnate devils throwing the milk that was warming for her infant on the dunghill, and the skillet in which it was contained into the cart, answering her prayers for mercy on her babe. Let the brat of a heretic starve.—ED.

QUESTION V.

WHAT MIGHT BE THE REASON MOVED GOD TO ORDAIN AND CHOOSE TO SAVE THOSE THAT HE SAVETH BY HIS GRACE, RATHER THAN BY ANY OTHER MEANS?

I come now to answer the fifth question; namely, to show why God saveth those that he saveth by grace, rather than by any other means.

First. God saveth us by grace, because since sin is in the world, he can save us no other way; sin and transgression cannot be removed but by the grace of God through Christ; sin is the transgression of the law of God, who is perfectly just. Infinite justice cannot be satisfied with the recompence that man can make; for if it could, Christ Jesus himself needed not to have died; besides, man having sinned, and defiled himself thereby, all his acts are the acts of a defiled man; nay, further, the best of his performances are also defiled by his hands; these performances, therefore, cannot be a recompence for sin. Besides, to affirm that God saveth defiled man for the sake of his defiled duties— for so, I say, is every work of his hand—what is it but to say, God accepteth of one sinful act as a recompence and satisfaction for another? (Hag. ii. 14). But God, even of old, hath declared how he abominates imperfect sacrifices, therefore we can by no means be saved from sin but by grace (Rom. iii. 24).

Second. To assert that we may be saved any other way than by the grace of God, what is it but to object against the wisdom and prudence of God, wherein he aboundeth towards them whom he hath saved by grace? (Eph. i. 5-8). His wisdom and prudence found out no other way, therefore he chooseth to save us by grace.

Third. We must be saved by grace, because else it follows that God is mutable in his decrees, for so hath he determined before the foundation of the world; therefore he saveth us not, nor chooseth to save us by any other way, than by grace (Eph. i. 3, 4; iii. 8-11; Rom. ix. 23).

Fourth. If man should be saved any other way than by grace, God would be disappointed in his design to cut off boasting from his creature; but God's design to cut off boasting from his creature cannot be frustrated or disappointed; therefore he will save man by no other means than by grace; he, I say, hath designed that no flesh should glory in his presence, and therefore he refuseth their works; 'Not of works, lest any man should boast.' 'Where is boasting then? It is excluded. By what law? of works? Nay; but by the law of faith' (Eph. ii. 8, 9; Rom. iii. 24-28).

Fifth. God hath ordained that we should be saved by grace, that he might have the praise and glory of our salvation; that we should be 'to the praise of the glory of his grace, wherein he hath made us accepted in the Beloved' (Eph. i. 6). Now God will not lose his praise, and his glory he will not give to another; therefore God doth choose to save sinners but by his grace.

Sixth. God hath ordained, and doth choose to save us by grace, because, were there another way apparent, yet this is the way that is safest, and best secureth the soul. 'Therefore it is of faith, that it might be by grace; to the end the promise [the promise of eternal inheritance,

(Heb. ix. 14-16)] might be sure to all the seed' (Rom. iv. 16). No other way could have been sure. This is evident in Adam, the Jews, and, I will add, the fallen angels, who being turned over to another way than grace, you see in short time what became of them.

To be saved by grace supposeth that God hath taken the salvation of our souls into his own hand; and to be sure it is safer in God's hand than ours. Hence it is called the salvation of the Lord, the salvation of God, and salvation, and that of God.

When our salvation is in God's hand, himself is engaged to accomplish it for us. 1. Here is the mercy of God engaged for us (Rom. ix. 15). 2. Here is the wisdom of God engaged for us (Eph. i. 7, 8). 3. Here is the power of God engaged for us (1 Peter i. 3-5). 4. Here is the justice of God engaged for us (Rom. iii. 24, 25). 5. Here is the holiness of God engaged for us (Psa. lxxxix. 30-35). 6. Here is the care of God engaged for us, and his watchful eye is always over us for our good (1 Peter v. 7; Isa. xxvii. 1-3).

What shall I say? Grace can take us into favour with God, and that when we are in our blood (Ezek. xvi. 7, 8). Grace can make children of us, though by nature we have been enemies to God (Rom. ix. 25, 26). Grace can make them God's people which were not God's people (1 Peter ii. 9, 10). Grace will not trust our own salvation in our own hands—'He putteth no trust in his saints' (Job xv. 15). Grace can pardon our ungodliness, justify us with Christ's righteousness; it can put the spirit of Jesus Christ within us, it can help us up when we are down, it can heal us when we are wounded, it can multiply pardons, as we, through frailty, multiply transgressions.

What shall I say? Grace and mercy are everlasting. They are built up for ever. They are the delight of God. They rejoice against judgment. And therefore it is the most safe and secure way of salvation, and therefore hath God chosen to save us by his grace and mercy rather than any other way (Isa. xliii. 25; Rom. iii. 24, 25;

Isa. xliv. 2, 4; Psa. xxxvii. 23; Luke x. 33, 34; Isa. lv. 7, 8; Psa. cxxxvi.; lxxxix. 2; Mal. iii. 18; James ii. 13).

Seventh. We must be saved by the grace of God, or else God will not have his will. They that are saved are 'predestinated unto the adoption of children by Jesus Christ to himself, according to the good pleasure of his will, to the praise of the glory of his grace' (Eph. i. 5, 6).

1. But if it be his will that men should be saved by grace, then to think of another way is against the will of God. Hence they that seek to establish their own righteousness are such as are accounted to stand out in defiance against, and that do not submit to, the righteousness of God—that is, to the righteousness that he hath willed to be that through which alone we are saved by grace (Rom. x. 3).

2. If it be his will that men should be saved through grace, then it is his will that men should be saved by faith in that Christ who is the contrivance of grace; therefore they that have sought to be justified another way have come short of, and perished notwithstanding, that salvation that is provided of God for men by grace (Rom. ix. 31-33).

3. God is not willing that faith should be made void, and the promise of none effect; therefore they of the righteousness of the law are excluded: 'for if the inheritance be of the law, it is no more of promise, but God gave it to Abraham by promise' (Rom. iv. 14 Gal. iii. 18).

4. God is not willing that men should be saved by their own natural abilities; but all the works of the law which men do to be saved by, they are the works of men's natural abilities, and are therefore called the work of the flesh, but God is not willing that men should be saved by these, therefore no way but by his grace (Rom. iv. 1; Gal. iii. 1-3; Phil. iii. 3).

Eighth. We must be saved by grace, or else the main pillars and foundations of salvation are not only shaken, but overthrown—to wit, election, the new covenant, Christ, and the glory of God; but these must not be overthrown; therefore we must be saved by grace.

1. Election, which layeth hold of men by the grace of God, God hath purposed that that shall stand—the election of God standeth sure; therefore men must be saved by virtue of the election of grace (Rom. ix. 11; 2 Tim. ii. 19).

2. The covenant of grace, that must stand—'Brethren, I speak after the manner of men. Though it be but a man's covenant, yet if it be confirmed [as this is, by the death of the testator, (Heb. ix. 16, 17)] no man disannulleth, or addeth thereto'; therefore man must be saved by virtue of a covenant of grace (Gal. iii. 15).

3. Christ, who is the gift of the grace of God to the world, he must stand, because he is a sure foundation, 'the same yesterday, to-day, and for ever'; therefore men must be saved by grace, through the redemption that is in Christ (Isa. xxviii. 16; Heb. xiii. 8).

4. God's glory, that also must stand; to wit, the glory of his grace; for that he will not give to another; therefore men must so be saved from the wrath to come, that in their salvation praise may redound to the glory of his grace.

Ninth. There can be but one will the master in our salvation; but that shall never be the will of man, but of God; therefore man must be saved by grace (John i. 13; Rom. ix. 16).

Tenth. There can be but one righteousness that shall save a sinner; but that shall never be the righteousness of men, but of Christ (therefore men must be saved by grace), that imputeth this righteousness to whom he will.

Eleventh. There can be but one covenant by which men must be saved; but that shall never be the covenant of the law, for the weakness and unprofitableness thereof; therefore men must be saved by the covenant of grace, by which God will be merciful to our unrighteousnesses, and our sins and iniquities will remember no more (Heb. viii. 6-13).

Postscript

A few words by way of use, and so I shall conclude.

THE FIRST USE.

First. Is the salvation of the sinner by the grace of God? Then here you see the reason why God hath not respect to the personal virtues of men in the bringing of them to glory. Did I say, personal virtues? How can they have any to Godward that are enemies to him in their minds by wicked works? Indeed, men one to another seem to be, some better, some worse, by nature, but to God they are all alike, dead in trespasses and sins.[20]

We will, therefore, state it again—Are men saved by grace? Then here you may see the reason why conversion runs at that rate among the sons of men, that none are converted for their good deeds, nor rejected for their bad, but even so many of both, and only so many, are brought home to God as grace is pleased to bring home to him.

1. None are received for their good deeds; for then they would not be saved by grace, but by works. Works and grace, as I have showed, are in this matter oppo-

---

20 How abasing and humbling to human pride is it thus to conceive, that all have sinned, and, in the sight of God, are hell-deserving. What! says the honourable man, must I take mercy upon no higher consideration than the thief on the cross? Or the highly virtuous dame, Must I sue for mercy upon the same terms as the Magdalene? The faithful answer to both is, YES, or you must perish.—ED.

site each to other; if he be saved by works, then not by grace; if by grace, then not by works (Rom. xi). That none are received of God for their good deeds is evident, not only because he declares his abhorrence of the supposition of such a thing, but hath also rejected the persons that have at any time attempted to present themselves to God in their own good deeds for justification. This I have showed you before.

2. Men are not rejected for their bad deeds. This is evident by Manasseh, by the murderers of our Lord Jesus Christ, by the men that you read of in the nineteenth of the Acts, with many others, whose sins were of as deep a dye as the sins of the worst of men (2 Chron. xxxiii. 2, 13; Acts ii. 23, 41; xix. 19).

Grace respecteth, in the salvation of a sinner, chiefly the purpose of God; wherefore those that it findeth under that purpose, those it justifies freely, through the redemption that is in Jesus Christ. At Saul's conversion, Ananias of Damascus brought in a most dreadful charge against him to the Lord Jesus Christ, saying, 'Lord, I have heard by many of this man, how much evil he hath done to thy saints at Jerusalem; and here he hath authority from the chief priests to bind all that call on thy name.' But what said the Lord unto him? 'Go thy way, for he is a chosen vessel unto me' (Acts ix. 13-15). This man's cruelty and outrage must not hinder his conversion, because he was a chosen vessel. Men's good deeds are no argument with God to convert them; men's bad deeds are no argument with him to reject them. I mean, those that come to Christ, by the drawings of the Father; besides, Christ also saith, 'I will in no wise cast' such 'out.' (John vi. 37-44).

Second. Is the salvation of the sinner by the grace of God? Then here you see the reason why some sinners, that were wonderfully averse to conversion by nature, are yet made to stoop to the God of their salvation. Grace takes them to do, because grace hath designed them to this very thing. Hence some of the Gentiles were taken from among the rest; God granted them repentance unto life, because he had taken them from among the rest, both by election and calling, for his name (Acts xi. 18; xv. 14). These men that were not a people, are thus become the people of God; these men that were not beloved for their works, were yet beloved by the grace of God. 'I will call them my people which were not my people; and her beloved which was not beloved.' But their minds are averse. But are they the people on whom God doth magnify the riches of his grace? Why, then, they shall be, in the day of his power, made willing, and be able to believe through grace (Psa. cx. 3; Rom. ix. 25; Acts xviii. 27). But doth the guilt and burden of sin so keep them down that they can by no means lift up themselves? Why, God will, by the exceeding greatness of that power by which he raised Christ from the dead, work in their souls also by the Spirit of grace, to cause them to believe and to walk in his ways (Eph. i. 18-20).

Paul tells us, in that epistle of his to the Corinthians, that it was by grace he was what he was—'By the grace of God I am what I am,' says he, 'and his grace which was bestowed upon me was not in vain' (1 Cor. xv. 10). This man kept always in his mind a warm remembrance of what he was formerly by nature, and also how he had added to his vileness by practice; yea, moreover, he truly concluded in his own soul, that had not God, by unspeakable grace, put a stop to his wicked proceedings, he had perished in his wickedness; hence he lays his call and conversion at the door of the grace of God—'When it pleased God,' says he, 'who separated me from my mother's womb, and called me by his grace, to reveal his Son in me' (Gal. i. 15, 16). and hence it is, again, that he saith, 'He obtained grace and apostleship'; grace to convert his soul, and the gifts and authority of an apostle, to preach the gospel of the grace of God.

This blessed man ascribes all to the grace of God. 1. His call he ascribes to the grace of God. 2. His apostleship he ascribes to the grace of God. 3. And all his labour in that charge he also ascribes to the grace of God.

This grace of God it was that which saved from the beginning. 1. Noah found grace in the eyes of the Lord, and was therefore converted and preserved from the flood (Gen. vi. 8). 2. Abraham found grace in the sight of the Lord, and therefore he was called out of his country (Gen. xii. 1, 2). 3. Moses found grace in the eyes of the Lord, and therefore he must not be blotted out of God's book (Exod. xxxiii. 12, 17).

Neither may it be imagined that these men were, before grace laid hold on them, better than other men; for then they would not have been saved by grace; grace should not have had the dominion and glory of their salvation. But, as Paul says of himself, and of those that were saved by grace in his day, 'What then? are we better than they? No, in no wise; for we have before proved both Jews and Gentiles that they are all under sin' (Rom. iii. 9). So it may be said of these blessed ones; for indeed this conclusion is general, and reacheth all the children of men, Christ Jesus alone only excepted. But,

Third. Is the salvation of the sinner by the grace of God? Then here you may see the reason why one backslider is recovered, and another left to perish in his backsliding.

There was grace for Lot, but none for his wife; therefore she was left in her transgression, but Lot was saved notwithstanding. There was grace for Jacob, but none for Esau; therefore Esau was left in his backsliding, but Jacob found mercy notwithstanding. There was grace for David, but none for Saul; therefore David obtained mercy, and Saul perished in his backsliding. There was grace for Peter, but none for Judas; therefore Judas is left to perish in his backsliding, and Peter is saved from his sin. That text stands good to none but those that are elect by grace—'Sin shall not have dominion over you; for ye are not under the law, but under grace' (Rom. vi. 14).

It will be said, repentance was found in one, but

not in the other. Well, but who granted and gave the one repentance; The Lord turned, and looked upon Peter; he did not turn and look upon Judas; yea, the Lord told Peter before he fell that he should follow him to the kingdom of heaven, but told him that he should deny him first; but withal told him also he should not let his heart be troubled, that is, utterly dejected, for he would go and prepare a place for him, and come again and receive him to himself (John xiii. 36-38; xiv. 1-3). That is a blessed word of God, 'The steps of a good man are ordered by the Lord, and he delighteth in his way. Though he fall, he shall not be utterly cast down; for the Lord upholdeth him with his hand' (Psa. xxxvii. 23, 24).

THE SECOND USE.

My second use shall be to them that are dejected in their souls at the sight and sense of their sins.

First. Are they that are saved, saved by grace? Then they that would have their guilty consciences quieted, they must study the doctrine of grace.

It is Satan's great design either to keep the sinner senseless of his sins, or if God makes him sensible of them, then to hide and keep from his thoughts the sweet doctrine of the grace of God, by which alone the conscience getteth health and cure; 'for everlasting consolation, and good hope' is given 'through grace' (1 Thess. ii. 16). How then shall the conscience of the burdened sinner by rightly quieted, if he perceiveth not the grace of God?

Study, therefore, this doctrine of the grace of God. Suppose thou hast a disease upon thee which is not to be cured but by such or such medicines, the first step to thy cure is to know the medicines. I am sure this is true as to the case in hand; the first step to the cure of a wounded conscience is for thee to know the grace of God, especially the grace of God as to justification from the curse in his sight.

A man under a wounded conscience naturally leaneth to the works of the law, and thinks God must be pacified by something that he should do, whereas the Word says, 'I will have mercy and not sacrifice: for I am not come to call the righteous, but sinners to repentance' (Matt. ix. 13).

Wherefore thou must study the grace of God. 'It is a good thing,' saith the apostle, 'that the heart be established with grace'; thereby insinuating that there is no establishment in the soul that is right but by the knowledge of the grace of God (Heb. xiii. 9).

I said, that when a man is wounded in his conscience, he naturally leaneth to the works of the law; wherefore thou must therefore be so much the more heedful to study the grace of God; yea, so to study it as rightly, not only in notion, but in thy practices, to distinguish it from the law. 'The law was given by Moses, but grace and truth came by Jesus Christ' (John i. 17). Study it, I say, so as to distinguish it, and that, not only from the law, but from all those things that men blasphemously call this grace of God.

There are many things which men call the grace of God, that are not.

1. The light and knowledge that are in every man. 2. That natural willingness that is in man to be saved. 3. That power that is in man by nature to do something, as he thinketh, towards his own salvation.

I name these three; there are also many other which some will have entitled the grace of God. But do thou remember that the grace of God is his goodwill and great love to sinners in his Son Jesus Christ; 'by the which' good 'will we are sanctified, through the offering of the body of Jesus Christ once for all' (Heb. x. 10).

Again; when thou hast smelt out this grace of God, and canst distinguish it from that which is not, then labour to strengthen thy soul with the blessed knowledge of it. 'Thou therefore, my son,' said Paul, 'be strong in the grace that is in Christ Jesus' (2 Tim. ii. 1). Fortify thy judgment and understanding; but especially labour to get down all into thy conscience, that that may be 'purged from dead works, to serve the living God.'

[Second.] And to enforce this use upon thee yet further, consider, a man gets yet more advantage by the knowledge of, and by growing strong in, this grace of God.

1. It ministereth to him matter of joy; for he that knows this grace aright, he knows God is at peace with him, because he believeth in Jesus Christ, who by grace tasted death for every man; 'by whom also we have access by faith into this grace wherein we stand, and rejoice in hope of the glory of God' (Rom. v. 2). And indeed what joy or what rejoicing is like rejoicing here? To rejoice in hope of the glory of God, it is to rejoice in hope to enjoy him for ever, with that eternal glory that is in him.

2. As it manifesteth matter of joy and rejoicing, so it causeth much fruitfulness in all holiness and godliness. 'For the grace of God that bringeth salvation hath appeared to all men, teaching us that, denying ungodliness and worldly lusts, we should live soberly, righteously, and godly in this present world' (Titus ii. 11, 12). Yea, it so naturally tendeth this way, that it can no sooner appear to the soul, but it causeth this blessed fruit in the heart and life. 'We ourselves also were sometimes foolish, disobedient, deceived, serving divers lusts and pleasures, living in malice and envy, hateful, and hating one another. But after that the kindness and love of God our Saviour appeared' — what then? Why then, he that believeth, being justified by his grace, and expecting to be an heir according to the hope of eternal life, is 'careful to maintain good works' (Titus iii. 3- 8). See also that in Paul's epistle to the Colossians—'We give thanks,' says he, 'to God and the Father of our Lord Jesus Christ, praying always for you, since we heard of your faith in Christ Jesus, and of the love which ye have to all the saints, for the hope which is laid up for you in heaven, whereof ye heard before in the word of the truth of the gospel; which is come unto you, as it is in all the world; and bringeth forth fruit, as it doth also in you, since the day ye heard of it, and knew the grace of

God in truth' (Col. i. 3-6).

3. The knowledge of, and strength that comes by, the grace of God is a sovereign antidote against all, and all manner of delusions that are or may come into the world. Wherefore Peter, exhorting the believers to take heed that they were not carried away with the errors of the wicked, and so fall from their own steadfastness, adds, as their only help, this exhortation—'But grow in grace, and in the knowledge of our Lord and Saviour Jesus Christ' (2 Peter iii. 18).

(1.) Suppose it should be urged, that man's own righteousness saveth the sinner; why, then, we have this at hand—God 'hath saved us, and called us, not according to our works, but according to his own purpose and grace, which was given us in Christ' &c. (2 Tim. i. 9).

(2.) Suppose it should be urged, that by the doctrine of free grace we must not understand God's extending free forgiveness as far as we have or do sin; the answer is—'But where sin abounded, grace did much more abound: that as sin hath reigned unto death, even so might grace reign through righteousness,' through the justice of God being satisfied by his Son, 'unto eternal life' (Rom. v. 20, 21).

(3.) Suppose it should be urged, that this is a doctrine tending to looseness and lasciviousness; the answer is ready—'What shall we say then? Shall we continue in sin, that grace may abound? God forbid. How shall we, that are dead to sin, live any longer therein?' for the doctrine of free grace believed is the most sin-killing doctrine in the world (Rom. vi. 1, 2).

(4.) Suppose men should attempt to burden the church of God with unnecessary ceremonies, and impose them, even as the false apostles[21] urged circumci-

---

21 'False apostles,' mentioned in Acts xv., who would have blended Jewish observances with Christianity, and have brought the converts into misery and thraldom. They are specially referred to in 2 Corinthians xi. 13, 'false apostles,' deceitful workers, that devour you and take from you (verse 20). In contradistinction to Paul, who was 'chargeable to no man' (verse 9).—ED.

sion of old, saying, Unless you do these things, ye cannot be saved; why, the answer is ready—'Why tempt ye God, to put a yoke upon the necks of the disciples, which neither our fathers nor we were able to bear? But we believe that through the grace of the Lord Jesus Christ we shall be saved, even as they' (Acts xv. 1, 10, 11). But not to enlarge,[22]

[Third.] This doctrine, 'By grace ye are saved,' it is the only remedy against despairing thoughts at the apprehension of our own unworthiness; as,

1. Thou criest out, O cursed man that I am! my sins will sink me into hell.

ANSW. Hold, man; there is a God in heaven that is 'the God of all grace' (1 Peter v. 10). Yet thou art not the man of all sin. If God be the God of all grace, then if all the sins in the world were thine, yet the God of all grace can pardon, or else it should seem that sin is stronger in a man penitent, to damn, than the grace of God can be to save.

2. But my sins are of the worst sort—blasphemy, adultery, covetousness, murder, &c.

ANSW. 'All manner of sins and blasphemy shall be forgiven unto men, wherewithsoever they shall blaspheme.—Let the wicked forsake his way, and the unrighteous man his thoughts; and let him return unto the Lord, and he will have mercy upon him; and to our God, for he will abundantly pardon' (Matt. xii. 31; Mark iii. 28; Isa. lv. 7, 8).

3. But I have a stout and rebellious heart, a heart that is far from good.

ANSW. 'Hearken unto me,' saith God, 'ye stout-hearted, that are far from righteousness: I bring near my righteousness'; that is, the righteousness of Christ, by

---

22 We must not for a moment imagine that Bunyan was afraid of temporal consequences, which prevents his enlarging upon this part of his subject. His contemptuous answer to Fowler for attacking the doctrine of justification, although a great man with the state, and soon afterwards made a bishop, is a proof that he was a stranger to the fear of man. He had said enough, and therefore there was no need to enlarge.—ED.

which stout-hearted sinners are justified, though ungodly (Isa. xlvi. 12, 13; Phil. iii. 7, 8; Rev. iv. 5).

4. But I have a heart as hard as any stone.

Answ. 'A new heart also will I give you,' says God, 'and a new spirit will I put within you: and I will take away the stony heart out of your flesh, and I will give you a heart of flesh' (Ezek. xxxvi. 26).

5. But I am as blind as a beetle; I cannot understand anything of the gospel.

Answ. 'I will bring the blind by a way that they know not; I will lead them in paths that they have not known: I will make darkness light before them, and crooked things straight. These things will I do unto them, and not forsake them' (Isa. xlii. 16).

6. But my heart will not be affected with the sufferings and blood of Christ.

Answ. 'I will pour upon the house of David, and upon the inhabitants of Jerusalem, the Spirit of grace and of supplications: and they shall look upon me whom they have pierced, and they shall mourn for him, as one mourneth for his only son, and shall be in bitterness for him, as one that is in bitterness for his firstborn' (Zech. xii. 10).

7. But though I see what is like to become of me if I find not Christ, yet my spirit, while I am thus, will be running after vanity, foolishness, uncleanness, wickedness.

Answ. 'Then will I sprinkle clean water upon you, and ye shall be clean: from all your filthiness, and from all your idols will I cleanse you' (Ezek. xxxvi. 25).

8. But I cannot believe in Christ.

Answ. But God hath promised to make thee believe. 'I will also leave in the midst of thee an afflicted and poor people, and they shall trust in the name of the Lord.' And again, 'There shall be a root of Jesse, and he that shall rise to reign over the Gentiles, in him shall the Gentiles trust' (Zeph. iii. 12; Rom. xv. 12).

9. But I cannot pray to God for mercy.

Answ. But God hath graciously promised a spirit

of prayer—'Yea, many people and strong nations shall come to seek the Lord of hosts in Jerusalem, and to pray before the Lord.—They shall call on my name, and I will hear them: I will say, It is my people; and they shall say, The Lord is my God' (Zech. viii. 22; xii. 10; xiii. 9).

10. But I cannot repent. ANSW. 'The God of our fathers raised up Jesus, whom ye slew and hanged on a tree. Him hath God exalted with his right hand to be a Prince and a Saviour, for to give repentance to Israel, and forgiveness of sins' (Acts v. 30, 31).

Thus might I enlarge, for the holy Bible is full of this exceeding grace of God. O these words, 'I will' and 'you shall'! they are the language of a gracious God; they are promises by which our God has engaged himself to do that for poor sinners which would else be left undone for ever.

THE THIRD USE.

Are they that are saved, saved by grace? Then let Christians labour to advance God's grace. FIRST. In heart. SECOND. In life.

FIRST. In heart; and that in this manner—

First. Believe in God's mercy through Jesus Christ, and so advance the grace of God; I mean, venture heartily, venture confidently, for there is a sufficiency in the grace of God. Abraham magnified the grace of God when 'he considered not his own body now dead, - neither yet the deadness of Sarah's womb: he staggered not at the promise of God through unbelief; but was strong in faith, giving glory to God' (Rom. iv. 19, 20).

Second. Advance it by heightening of it in thy thoughts. Have always good and great thoughts of the grace of God; narrow and slender thoughts of it are a great disparagement to it.

And to help thee in this matter, consider—1. This grace is compared to a sea—'And thou wilt cast all their sins into the depths of the sea' (Micah vii. 19). Now a sea can never be filled by casting into it.[23]

2. This grace is compared to a fountain, to an open fountain—'In that day there shall be a fountain opened to the house of David, and to the inhabitants of Jerusalem, for sin and for uncleanness.' Now a fountain can never be drawn dry (Zech. xii. 1). 3. The Psalmist cries out concerning the grace and mercy of God, 'It endureth for ever'; he says so twenty-six times in one psalm. Surely he saw a great deal in it, surely he was taken a great deal with it (Psa. cxxxvi.). 4. Paul says the God of all grace can do more than 'we ask or think' (Eph. iii. 20). 5. Therefore as God's Word says, so thou shouldst conclude of the grace of God.

Third. Come boldly to the throne of grace by hearty prayer; for this is the way also to magnify the grace of God. This is the apostle's exhortation, 'Let us therefore come boldly unto the throne of grace, that we may obtain mercy, and find grace to help in time of need' (Heb. iv. 16). See here a little, and wonder.

We have been all this while discoursing of the grace of God; and now we are come to his throne, as Job says, 'even to his seat'; and behold, 'that is a throne of grace.' O, when a God of grace is upon a throne of grace, and a poor sinner stands by and begs for grace, and that in the name of a gracious Christ, in and by the help of the Spirit of grace, can it be otherwise but such a sinner must obtain mercy and grace to help in time of need? But not to forget the exhortation, 'Come boldly.' Indeed, we are apt to forget this exhortation; we think, seeing we are such abominable sinners, we should not presume to come boldly to the throne of grace; but yet so we are bidden to do; and to break a commandment here is as bad as to break it in another place.

You may ask me, What is it to come boldly? [I] answer—

1. It is to come confidently—'Let us draw near with

---

23 How does Bunyan here exhibit the perfection as well as the freeness of the pardon that Micah celebrates! That which is sunk in the depths of the sea is lost for ever.—Ed.

a true heart, in full assurance of faith, having our hearts sprinkled from an evil conscience, and our bodies washed with pure water' (Heb. x. 22).

2. To come boldly, it is to come frequently—'At morning, at noon, and at night, will I pray.' We use to count them bold beggars that come often to our door.

3. To come boldly, it is to ask for great things when we come. That is the bold beggar that will not only ask, but also choose the thing that he asketh.

4. To come boldly, it is to ask for others as well as ourselves, to beg mercy and grace for all the saints of God under heaven as well as for ourselves—'Praying always with all prayer and supplication in the Spirit - for all saints' (Eph. vi. 18).

5. To come boldly, it is to come and take no nay; thus Jacob came to the throne of grace—'I will not let thee go except thou bless me' (Gen. xxxii. 26).

6. To come boldly, it is to plead God's promises with him both in a way of justice and mercy, and to take it for granted God will give us—because he hath said it—whatever we ask in the name of his Son.

Fourth. Labour to advance God's grace in thy heart, by often admiring, praising, and blessing God in secret for it; God expects it— 'Whoso offereth praise glorifieth me,' says he. 'By Jesus Christ therefore let us offer the sacrifice of praise to God continually; that is, the fruit of our lips, giving thanks to his name' (Psa. l. 23; Heb. xiii. 15).

SECOND. [In life.] But again; as we should advance this grace in our hearts, so we should do it in our life. We should in our conversation adorn the doctrine of God our Saviour in all things. It is a great word of the apostle, 'Only let your conversation be as it becometh the gospel of Christ,' which is the gospel of the grace of God (Phil. i. 27). God expecteth that there should in our whole life be a blessed tang[24] of the gospel, or that in

---

24 'Tang,' taste, touch, savour, flavour, relish, tone, sound. A word of extensive meaning, but now nearly obsolete. 'No tang of prepossession or fancy appears in the morality of our Saviour or

our life among men there should be preached to them the grace of the gospel of God.

The gospel shows us that God did wonderfully stoop and condescend for our good; and to do accordingly, it is to stoop and condescend to others.

The gospel shows us that there was abundance of pity, love, bowels, and compassion in God towards us; and accordingly we should be full of bowels, pity, love, and compassion to others.

The gospel shows us that in God there is a great deal of willingness to do good to others.

The gospel shows us that God acteth towards us according to his truth and faithfulness, and so should we be in all our actions one to another.

By the gospel, God declares that he forgiveth us ten thousand talents, and we ought likewise to forgive our brother the hundred pence.

And now, before I conclude this use, let me give you a few heart- endearing considerations to this so good and so happy a work.

[Heart-endearing Considerations.]

First. Consider, God hath saved thee by his grace. Christian, God hath saved thee, thou hast escaped the lion's mouth, thou art delivered from wrath to come; advance the grace that saves thee, in thy heart and life.

Second. Consider, God left millions in their sins that day he saved thee by his grace; he left millions out, and pitched upon thee; it may be hundreds also, yea, thousands, were in the day of thy conversion lying before him under the preaching of the word as thou wert, yet he took thee.[25] Considerations of this nature affected David much; and God would have them affect thee, to the advancing of his grace in thy life and conversation

---

his apostles.'—Locke.—Ed.

25 What can I render unto thee, my God, for such unspeakable blessedness? The cattle upon a thousand hills, yea, all creation, all that I have and am, is thine: all that I can do is 'to take the cup of salvation and call upon the name of the Lord.' Not unto us, but unto thy name, be all the praise and honour of salvation!—Ed.

(Psa. lxxviii. 67-72; Deut. vii. 7).

Third. Consider, perhaps the most part of those that God refused that day that he called thee by his grace were, as to conversation, far better than ever thou wert—I was a blasphemer, I was a persecutor, I was an injurious person, but I obtained mercy! O this should affect thy heart, this should engage thy heart to study to advance this grace of God (1 Tim. i. 14, 15).

Fourth. Perhaps in the day of thy conversion thou wast more unruly than many. Like a bullock unaccustomed to the yoke, hardly tamed, thou wast brought home by strong hands; thou wouldst not drive, the Lord Jesus must take thee up, lay thee upon his shoulder, and carry thee home to his Father's house. This should engage thy heart to study to advance the grace of God (Luke xv. 1-6).

Fifth. It may be many did take even offence at God in his converting and saving of thee by his grace, even as the elder son was offended with his father for killing the fatted calf for his brother, and yet that did not hinder the grace of God, nor make God abate his love to thy soul. This should make thee study to advance the grace of God in thy heart and life (Luke xv. 21-32).

Sixth. Consider again, that God hath allowed thee but a little time for this good work, even the few days that thou hast now to live—I mean, for this good work among sinful men, and then thou shalt go to receive that wages that grace also will give thee for thy work to thy eternal joy.

Seventh. Let this also have some place upon thy heart—every man shows subjection to the god that he serveth; yea, though that god be none other but the devil and his lusts; and wilt not thou, O man! saved of the Lord, be much more subject 'to the Father of spirits, and live'?[26]

---

26 In the edition of 1692, this sentence is 'subject to the Father of spirits and love.' It is a very singular mode of expression to call God 'the Father of love.' God is love, and that author and source of all holy love. Bunyan was at all times governed by Scripture

Alas! they are pursuing their own damnation, yet they sport it, and dance all the way they go. They serve that 'god' (Satan) with cheerfulness and delight, who at last will plunge them into the everlasting gulf of death, and torment them in the fiery flames of hell; but thy God is the God of salvation, and to God thy Lord belong the issues from death. Wilt not thou serve him with joyfulness in the enjoyment of all good things, even him by whom thou art to be made blessed for ever?

OBJECT. This is that which kills me—honour God I cannot; my heart is so wretched, so spiritless, and desperately wicked, I cannot.

ANSW. What dost thou mean by cannot? 1. If thou meanest thou hast no strength to do it, thou hast said an untruth, for 'greater is he that is in you, than he that is in the world' (1 John iv. 4). 2. If thou meanest thou hast no will, then thou art out also; for every Christian, in his right mind, is a willing man, and the day of God's power hath made him so (Psa. cx. 3). 3. If thou meanest that thou wantest wisdom, that is thine own fault—'If any man lack wisdom, let him ask of God, that giveth to all men liberally, and upbraideth not' (James i. 5).

OBJECT. I cannot do things as I would.

ANSW. No more could the best of the saints of old—'To will is present with me,' said Paul; 'but how to perform that which is good I find not.' And again, 'The flesh lusteth against the Spirit, and the Spirit against the flesh: and these are contrary the one to the other, so that ye cannot do the things that ye would' (Rom. vii. 18; Gal. v. 17).

And here indeed lies a great discovery of this truth, 'ye are saved by grace'; for the children of God whilst here, notwithstanding their conversion to God, and sal-

---

phrases, with which his mind was so richly imbued as to cause him, if we may so speak, to live in a scriptural atmosphere; and this sentence bears a great affinity to Hebrews xii. 9, 'Shall we not much rather be in subjection to the Father of spirits, and live.' I have been, for these reasons, induced to consider the letter o in 'love' a typographical error, and have altered the word to 'live,' but could not take such a liberty without a public notice.—ED.

vation by Christ through grace, are so infirm and weak by reason of a body of death that yet remaineth in them, that should even the sin that is in the best of their performances be laid to their charge, according to the tenor of a covenant of works, they would find it impossible ever to get into glory. But why do I talk thus? It is impossible that those that are saved by grace should have their infirmities laid to their charge as afore, 'for they are not under the law'; they are included by the grace of God in the death and blood of the Son of God, who ever liveth to make intercession for them at the right hand of God; whose intercession is so prevalent with the Father as to take away the iniquity of our holy things from his sight, and to present us holy, and unreprovable, and unblamable in his sight. To him, by Christ Jesus, through the help of the blessed Spirit of grace, be given praise, and thanks, and glory, and dominion, by all his saints, now and for ever. Amen.

www.ingramcontent.com/pod-product-compliance
Lightning Source LLC
Chambersburg PA
CBHW012107090526
44592CB00019B/2681